soul 2 soul

soul 2 soul

CHRISTOPHER L. COPPERNOLL

WORD PUBLISHING
NASHVILLE
A Thomas Nelson Company

Published by Word Publishing, a unit of Thomas Nelson, Inc., P.O. Box 141000, Nashville, Tennessee 37214.

ISBN: 1-56865-985-7

Printed in the United States of America

To my parents,
Bob and Lois Coppernoll—
for your sacrifice
your devotion and love

CONTENTS

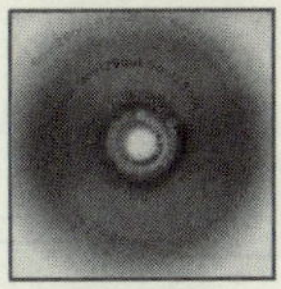

Contents

FOREWORD

We learn so much from each other's stories. The impact of monologues proffered from the lecture halls of academia cannot begin to compare with the power of a heart recounting tales from the variegated journey we call life. So much of God's Word comes to us in the form of storytelling. In both the Old and New Testament narratives we are encouraged and challenged as we enter into the heartache of sin and the joy of redemption as the history of salvation is so creatively and faithfully preserved for us. Pretty soon we realize that these stories are really our stories because we are a part of the same family and the same tapestry of failure and grace. Such is the power of stories.

In this same tradition Chris Coppernoll has given us a good gift through the years in his program called *Soul2Soul.* By demythologizing the talented men and women of contemporary Christian music, he has given us a window into our own souls. Because of his own commitment to wrestle with the implications of the grace of God, Chris has enabled many artists to feel comfortable in sharing with us their stories of fear, joy, foolishness, and growth. Through their vulnerability, each of us is given the same opportunity to own our brokenness and to celebrate the sufficiency of the love of our Savior.

God has given Chris a very unique gift of asking the right questions which segue into some pretty amazing disclosures and dialogue with our friends who make so much of the music which enriches our worship of God and understanding of the life of faith. It is my privilege and calling to pastor many of these gifted individuals, including Chris. I recommend to you not only these written accounts of many of the special moments from *Soul2Soul*, I also commend Chris to you. He is a friend whose own story and heart have invited me to drink more deeply from the fountain of God's grace.

Pastor Scotty Smith
Christ Community Church
Franklin, Tennessee

ACKNOWLEDGMENTS

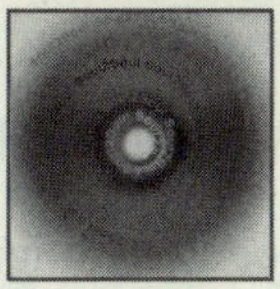

Writing this book has been an exercise in prayer and trust. My desire is that you will feel connection with our Lord and Savior Jesus Christ and with these believers we call contemporary Christian artists. This author owes a considerable debt of gratitude to each of these people for helping shape Soul2Soul.

- Our instrumental group of friends and supporters who believed before there was much to see: Bob & Merrill Farnsworth, Jill Landess, Pamela Muse, Jessica Atteberry, Barbara King, Victoria Aebischer, Terry Todd and the staff at Benson Music Group, Andrew Tempest, Jeff Brown, Michelle Younkman and the staff at Myrrh Records, Chris Hauser, Kevin Killingsworth, Michelle Fink, Therese Romano, the staff at Reunion Records, Missy Baker and the staff at Damascus Road, Rodney Hatfield and the staff at Spring Hill, Chris Redner, Lindy Warren, Brian Smith and the staff at Turning Point Media Relations.

- Our team in radio production both past and present for *Soul2Soul* and *Soul2Soul Journal*: Mike & Natalie Becht, Troy & Wendy Smith, Jack & Sherri Fussell, Kerith Harding, Diane Williamson, and the staff at ProAudio, Inc in New Albany, Indiana.

- My literary agents Michael Hyatt, Robert Wolgemuth and the staff at Wolgemuth & Associates.

- Everyone at Word Publishing: Lee Gessner, Ami McConnell, Pamela McClure, and Janet Rowland.

- Pastor Scotty Smith and Christ Community Church in Franklin, Tennessee.

- The men and women who work in Christian radio everywhere.

- The artists who have graced our microphone for the past four years. Your generosity is boundless. Thank you for your music and striving to let your character be your lyric. Thanks to countless artists' managers for your assistance in bringing these artists together for this book.

- My wife, Lori, and my daughter, Gray. My parents and my family. I love you.

- My Lord and Savior Jesus Christ who alone deserves all glory.

1 THE CALLING

> **"There are many ways to discuss the doctrines of Christianity; but when it comes to living the Christian life, I have come to believe that each man has only one story to tell."**
>
> **Keith Miller, The Taste of New Wine**

A LIFE "CALLED BY GOD"—it's an outrageous concept when you stop to think about it. When I ponder all this expression might mean, my brain ends up feeling as fried as that egg in the "brain on drugs" commercial.

Called by God. Just what does that mean?

After some serious thought, I'm tempted to pick up my trusty Louisville Slugger (er, pen that is) and take a big ol' whack at this cryptic, yet often used saying. "Called"—could it mean "chosen" by God for a particular role? Of course it might mean "prepared" by God to perform a specific task. Or it may even mean "designed" by God to be whatever a person becomes. Whatever the definition, a calling is always accompanied by a strong, inner urge to do what is compelling us.

My curiosity about "the calling" placed on contemporary Christian music artists transpired during the hundred or so interviews I've conducted with Christian music artists during the past three years. During most of these interviews invariably I found myself asking the interviewee: "At your deepest level, just what makes you do this?" After hearing a few dozen answers, a glimmer of commonality surfaced in the artists' stories. Their shared backgrounds, similar explanations, and early understandings of purpose clearly marked their biographies like signposts along I-40 heading into Nashville.

I wondered, *Is God calling, equipping, and using contemporary Christian artists to carry out His work within the body of the Church?*

This idea that God would use singers to convey His message has proven to be a major hurdle for some within the Church. Much skepticism has been expressed over the years concerning the calling of Gospel artists, their role within the Church, and the overall usefulness of Christian music. Testimonies in this chapter provide candid insights into these matters for anyone who may be asking these kinds of important questions.

Personally, I believe God is calling all who will seek Him. Even if we are not called to be Christian recording artists, these stories are reminders for us to be on the lookout for our own calling.

So how does a Christian artist get to be a Christian artist? Is it calling or coincidence, nature or nurture, drive or destiny? With more than two billion career choices available, they chose this one. Or did they?

Twila Paris

> We didn't have a home when I was young; we literally traveled all the time until I was 7 years old. My dad was a traveling evangelist and we would go to one church, stay for two weeks, and then to another for two more. I went to church every single night and heard my dad preach. I can remember very clearly one night when I was 4 years old my dad gave an invitation. It was then that I went down and accepted Jesus Christ as Savior. I believe that decision had validity. Of course a conversion—a true commitment to Christ—must grow up because we add a lot of dimensions to our lives.

Obviously, ministry is a calling for me, and I think music was too. It was a gift that God placed in me, a desire He placed in my heart because He wanted me to use it in a particular way. But like a lot of gifts, this one rose out of my ministry and my relationship with God.

In high school I knew I wanted to be involved in music as a vocation somehow. Whether I would be a choir teacher or what I didn't know, but I knew I loved music. But at that point in my life, I loved it too much. I had to go through a time of willingness to give it up, lay it down, and do something else. I spent two or three years doing just that.

Right out of high school, I went through discipleship training with Youth with a Mission. During that time, two interesting things happened simultaneously. First, I came to the place where I was willing to do something besides music. That was important. Second, because of the things God was doing in my heart, *I began to write songs.* It was just as an outlet at first, a way to express those things I was learning. I was slowly getting rid of that "self-righteous preacher kid thing" and learning to really develop God's character in a true and pure way.

This went on for two or three years. I kept writing, and I had this growing stack of songs that I played only for my friends. I was believing more and more that God was never going to use my music. I thought maybe I would lead worship at home fellowship on Sunday nights and do something local, but not something full-time. But God was using this time as a training ground.

As every worship leader has experienced, sometimes we'll search for just the right song to fit in the worship service, and we can't find it. When that happened to me, I'd write the song I needed to use in our home fellowship. I wrote "We Will Glorify" in this situation. Because I wasn't recording at the time, a lot of the early worship songs that

I wrote were tested on *real people* before they were ever released.

As in the parable of the potter and the clay, over time God reshaped Twila's love for music until she could serve Him in the way that He wanted. When she looked to fill the need in her local body, she wound up writing songs that have ministered to countless churches all across the world.

Sometimes God gives us a vision to prepare us for His plans for our lives. In 1996, Clay Crosse sang a duet with Gospel patriarch Andrae Crouch at the 27th Annual Dove Awards. As the country watched, I thought back to this story Clay once told about himself as an undiscovered talent in Memphis, watching other Christian artists perform on stage.

Clay Crosse

I was pretty much just a normal kid growing up in Memphis, Tennessee. I did all the normal things like playing ball and going to school. I remember feeling really fortunate to be a part of a great youth group at my church. I was raised in a Christ-centered environment in my home where Christ was always the focus. I don't take those things for granted. Had it not been for these influences in my life, I wonder where I'd be today.

I didn't start singing until I was in my late teens. I sang a solo in church, and I was so nervous that I didn't think I ever wanted to do it again. Still, the more I sang, the more I realized this was something I wanted to do. I found I liked to sing in front of people. I started singing in groups in high school and then in college.

Then I landed a job singing at a theme park called Liberty Land. The first year I was in a Country/Western show, which isn't me at all! The next summer I was in a patriotic, all-American show. It was grueling. We performed four shows a day, six days a week. It was just crazy, but a very important time as far as getting some experience in front of people. But as the summer went on I felt like I was just spinning my wheels. I wasn't really being heard.

Around Easter 1991, I saw an ad in the paper for a solo concert by Gary McSpadden. I knew Gary used to sing with Bill Gaither and several other groups, so I said to my wife, Renna, "Why don't we go and see if we can't meet him and slip him a demo tape . . . who knows?" As it turns out, we did get to meet him and I got the tape into his hands. Gary was nice. I didn't know if he'd listened to my tape or not until his son called me a few days later. Wow, I can still remember getting that call on my answering machine and just being so happy. He was just wondering what I wanted to do with my life. He said that my voice had a certain magic to it, and he wanted to talk to me a little bit about it. I can remember thinking that it was the first time I'd met someone in the music business and being very excited. After getting to know the McSpaddens a little bit, I signed a management deal with them. A year or so after that we got the record deal at Reunion and things have just been smoking ever since.

It's interesting, before I was signed to my record deal, I was in the Young Messiah choir in Memphis. In every city where the tour goes, they put together a choir made up of the people in that city. And in Memphis that year, my wife and I were in that choir. I distinctly remember looking up on stage at Larnelle [Harris] and Sandi [Patty] and thinking it would be a dream come true to be a part of the Young Messiah tour. In 1995, that dream became a reality.

Now it just amazes me, looking back, that the Lord opened so many doors for me. I always felt that God had given me a talent, but I didn't know exactly why. I don't for a minute stand here and think I did this. I don't think because of my talent or because of some decisions that I made things have happened the way they have. I just think He's done it all for me. I try to keep that attitude, feeling totally dependent on Christ and giving Him all the glory. That's what I try to do. I thought maybe I had a chance of making a record one day or being involved with Christian music, but I didn't think it would come to this. I've never had visions of huge success.

No Christian recording artist has impacted the Christian music community as Amy Grant has. I've heard numerous unsolicited accounts from other Christian artists who have been inspired by Amy's talent and her character. When I heard this story about when she was "discovered," I found myself thinking of the game Mouse Trap. You know, the ball rolls down the shoot, falls through a narrow hole, barely knocks over the pail, and just allows the ringing of the bell. It's even more amazing watching it in real life.

Amy Grant

I knew Brown [Bannister] because we went to the same church. He was a dear friend. I had made a tape with about a dozen songs at a college studio here in Nashville. I made the tape for my mom and dad because I'd written a bunch of songs, and I didn't know how to write them down. I was beginning to forget the early songs the more I wrote. Brown was about ten years older than I, and he had a *real job* in a recording studio. Even though he had studio time because he was taking college classes, he didn't need it so he gave it to me.

So I made this dinky little tape. I had a friend of mine play piano, and I played guitar. Once I made it I really regretted it, because it sounded awful to me. My parents would invite somebody over and then they'd close the doors to the study and I'd hear that tape on in the study. I'd be up in my room thinking, *Oh dear God, rescue that poor couple who have come in.* My parents are so kind and gentle I don't think anyone would ever say, "We *really* have to go."

There was only the one copy of the tape, so I gave it to Brown and said, "Would you mind taking this to the studio where you work and just dubbing two or three copies?" He was doing it at an off time when nobody was going to be in the studio. It just so happened Brown's college buddy who worked in the music industry walked into the studio. His name was Chris Christian and I had met him before.

Chris said, "Who is this singing?"

Brown said, "That's Amy," and I think Chris said, "You're kidding?" He said, "Well, she's not great, but she certainly is sincere." I don't know if it was at that moment or if it was the next day, but Chris called Stan Moser, who was at Word Records at the time, and he played my tape over the phone. Stan told Chris, "Well, if you think she's got it . . . sign her."

Well, the way it all came down to me, it was a school night and my phone rang sometime after ten o'clock (which is a really normal time for a studio person to call). Brown was calling to say, "Hey, you're not going to believe this—Word Records wants to offer you a contract!" *I thought it was a joke.* I thought he was making fun of me. Right about the time he's really letting me know he's serious about the record deal, my father picks up the phone. *"You know it's after curfew time. Come downstairs right away."* So I hung up the phone. I was offered a record deal and got grounded at the same time. I don't even think I told my dad that I'd been offered a record deal because I was mad at him for grounding me.

Sometimes a vision of where we belong comes to us directly, and sometimes it comes from the people closest to us. In Pam Thum's case, she heard the calling coming from the voice of someone she most trusted.

Pam Thum

My daddy's a missionary evangelist, and my mom's a musician. I started singing when I was 2 years old. I even made an album when I was 3. My mom especially encouraged me to be creative and so at 10 I started writing my first songs.

I wrote kid songs like "I Want to Jog for Jesus (*and Do Push-ups in His Word*)"and just fun stuff like that. Later, as I matured in my writing and took it more seriously, I wrote "Hallelujah Praise the Lamb" and "We Are an Army."

Even though I was unknown, I was introduced to Gary and Carolyn McSpadden. They took me under their wing and told me *they believed in me*. I can remember all of us crying on the bus. We were praying, and they said "God's got His hand on you, Pam. We believe you're not just suppose to write: God wants you to be an artist and sing as well." I was just overwhelmed because I had always really looked up to Gary. I opened my eyes and watched them praying for me. I thought, *They feel like this is God's plan for my life*. I had felt that before, too, but really didn't know for sure. This confirmed it for me. Shortly after that experience their son took over my career, and I was signed to a record deal.

One of the themes that I see in so many interviews is that of families passing on their faith and ministry to their children. Here Greg Long tells not only how God prepared him, but how God prepared his parents a generation before.

Greg Long

I grew up traveling. When I was 6 months old, my father had just graduated from Bible college and he and my mother would hold revivals around the country. My mom and dad would sing at these revivals, and before long, I began to sing also. I think "Jesus Loves Me" was the first song I ever performed. I was 2.

My dad was the guy next door who God just happened to call to be an evangelist. He was so close to his family that he couldn't bear to leave us all behind. He just counted on taking us with him, and so off we went. When I was about 3 1/2, my other brother came along and we just continued to travel.

My grandparents lived on a little dairy farm in the hills outside of a place called Sisseton, South Dakota. That's the place we would go back to, and it's where I call home. But 250 to 300 days of the year, for all of my childhood, we were out on the road as a ministry family, holding revivals in churches.

It was a different life from the lives I guess a lot of people have. For example, for my entire school education I was tutored. A tutor would travel along with us who could also play the piano or sing during the nightly revival. Sometimes we would go for a year or two at a time without a tutor. In those times, my mom would teach all of us boys: myself, my younger brother Grayson, and my youngest brother, Grady.

I believe whom God calls, He enables. Take my mom for example: She's the mother of three boys; add in a husband and that makes four guys and one woman all traveling in one small camper. For 300 days a year that was her only home. Although that's not an easy life, I never heard a word of complaint from her. In 1997 my mom and dad celebrated their thirtieth year of full-time ministry.

Did God call her? I don't know, but I know He prepared her.

Had I never been signed to a recording contract with Myrrh Records, I would still be singing at churches, just as I am with a record contract. Sure, my responsibilities have changed a little. Now there are radio interviews to do, press to meet with, and the music's a little better, but this is just literally an extension of what I've been doing all of my life.

I find I'm like my dad. I've looked to my parents as teaching examples of how to do this thing that we do. My dad talks to people about what God has done in his life, and that's pretty much what I do. We're just average people that God has called to do this.

Just average people. Pastors tell us they are whom God usually calls. Erin O'Donnell is a new Christian artist who received considerable notoriety when she became the first performer to land a recording contract over the Internet. She took an interest in singing early on in life, but the calling of how to use her talent came much later. God leads us through specific circumstances to bring us right where He wants us to be.

Erin O'Donnell

I grew up in the Church and always went to church, but I never really paid too much attention to what was going on during the service. That's probably really terrible. I remember singing in the choir and feeling really worshipful when I was singing. I always felt close to God during those moments. But as for the rest of it, I was just kind of lost in the shuffle.

When I went away to college at the University of Miami, I was the only person who attended from my high school, and I felt all alone. I remember the first week of school my freshman year.

I didn't know anybody and the campus was so huge. I was sitting in my dorm room just crying when I stumbled across a Christian radio station, WMCU in Miami. I had never heard Christian music before. After I found that station I started playing it all the time. I don't even know why. I think it just made me feel less lonely there at school. I had this Walkman of mine on 24 hours a day walking to and from class and everywhere.

It's such a privilege to be able to do what I'm doing now because, looking back, I see how God used Christian radio to open my heart. If someone would have said at that time, "You need to come to this Bible study, or you need to do this or that," I don't think I would have paid a lot of attention, because my heart simply wasn't ready for it.

But through that opening, through the music, God really softened my heart. Then my roommate became a Christian and kept encouraging me to go to her Bible study. I thought she was a little "nuts" at the time! But eventually she got the Bible study moved to our apartment. I would come home and there would be twenty-five people sitting in a circle after classes holding a Bible study. Eventually I sat down, too, and started paying attention. Then in my sophomore year, I was led to Christ.

Originally I went to college only to pursue a degree in music. I ended up becoming a Christian, meeting my husband, Brad (he was the one leading the Bible study with a friend), and after playing music in Miami for quite a few years, being signed to a Christian record deal.

Brad and I never thought we'd be working together or doing anything like this. We met our record label on the Internet of all places, and we hooked up with them after we'd made a demo CD. We sent it to them at a P.O. Box in Tennessee, and two weeks later the president flew down to Miami to see us perform live. Four weeks after that we were signed, and four months later we were making our first record.

Erin O'Donnell's story of God's fine-tuning her direction in life makes us aware of both His patience and His gentle guidance. Like the prodigal son, experiences away from the Father guided Charlie Peacock to find what he was looking for.

Charlie Peacock

I grew up in Yuba City, California, population 14,000. I have lots of memories of being a kid there. Some of my best memories are when I used to stay at my grandmother's house when my parents were young. They both worked a lot at that time. My mom worked at the high school and my dad was a telephone lineman, he played trumpet in bands in little clubs at night, and he was also going to school. So I ended up staying with my Grandma a lot. She lived out in the country where there were lots of places to explore, trees to climb in, and chickens.

My interest in music started with wanting to be the next Beatles and wanting to do what my father did. I think my dad saw enough talent in me to want to cultivate it a little bit, but he was a real perfectionist. It was difficult for him to teach me.

My first instrument was a pair of drum sticks and a practice pad. My second instrument was the clarinet, then the cornet. I went through the band program at school and took music theory in high school. I also took it at the school my father taught at during summer school. It was the kind of thing where if I was working on music I could come to my dad and ask him questions. That was a pretty good way to go. But if he was actually trying to teach me or work with me on a piece of music, that was usually pretty difficult.

Once I started buying my own music, I got into it really deep. I would ride my bike to town to buy the latest records and I listened to top 40 music a lot. Probably from 1968 to 1973 I listened to the radio constantly, especially when I would go to sleep at night. I'd put my AM radio under my pillow and go to sleep listening to the hits of the day. In between eighth grade and my freshman year of high school I really discovered jazz. I started listening to my dad's jazz records, finding out more and more about different players, and buying a lot of jazz albums. At the time I was listening to singer-songwriters like James Taylor and Jackson Browne, but I was also listening to what was the early rock-jazz movement: electric Miles Davis, Chick Corea, things like that.

From the time I was 20 years old, people started to recognize in me the possibility that I could be a "pop star" and started investing time and money in me towards that end.

In those days I was not a Christian. I had gotten married when I was 18. I went down to L.A. and San F rancisco a lot, recording and basically traveling the path that you take to make it in the secular music world. I was always real close to getting something good happening, but at the same time I had a ravaging drug and alcohol habit. I had a lot of worldly experience with the kind of sin and vice that is often characterized as the "rock-and-roll lifestyle." I just kind of bought into all that. I had a lot of intrinsic, intellectual ability which was lying dormant because of what I was doing to my mind and body. So I really didn't have any kind of life of the mind at all. I was just driven by passion and selfish physical need. I hadn't given much thought to life except in how it might serve my wants and appetites.

There came a time shortly before my twenty-fifth birthday when the sum of my choices caved in on me. I was right in the middle of one of those "great opportunities," working with a record producer in San Francisco, but my life was absolutely a mess. Frankly, nobody really wanted to be around me unless they could gain something from me. The people whom I really loved had determined that there was nothing to be gained by enabling me, so I didn't see my parents or my wife or even my little children much. It was just a very painful time.

I just couldn't believe that my best efforts at living had brought me to the place of dependence on drugs or alcohol. I was really disgusted with myself and found that the only way to deal with it was to kind of anesthetize my pain further through the very things that were actually killing me. It was a vicious merry-go-round.

My music was getting worse as well. It seemed that every time I sat down to write, I was writing the same song. Really a person with talent is only as good as the ideas behind what they do and most of my ideas were either insufficient or untruthful. After my conversion to Christ, I had a reason to sing. I had the truth in my heart and was blossoming into a person dedicated to Christ.

When I was a freshman in high school, I had made a profession of faith in Christ, but my commitment was very, very short-lived. I thought at the time I wanted to go to Bible college and perhaps become a pastor. Then I made some other choices, choices based on genuine love for a girl, ones which were contradictory to my professed faith in Jesus. I had to choose and I chose sin. So for the next ten years of my life I walked outside of Christ, and God let me go. He gave me enough rope to hang myself, and I certainly did.

Being an artist, I was keenly aware of a spiritual dimension, but I felt that having left Christianity, there was now no returning to it. I felt I couldn't live up to it. I had a false notion of what Christianity was. I was trying to work my way to God. All I can say is it's God's grace and His sovereignty that brought me back. Somehow I knew that if I were going to start to pray again, that I would pray to the God of the Bible. So that's what I did. I started praying every morning and every night and many, many times during the day.

I had quite a foul mouth at that time and every other word was the "f" word. I would sit at my piano working on something and I wanted to drink *so bad* I would be cussing and then I would stop myself and pray to God, "*Please, help me, help me through this moment because I can't make it, I can't do it. I want to throw my life away. That's really what I want. I would throw my life away right now to have a fix to deal with my pain.*" I prayed to God for an entire year.

After a year at this I played a gig, one which I would have been too prideful to do in the past. I guess God had already started to break down some of that pride. I went and did this jazz, pseudo-cocktail gig at the top of the Holiday Inn in Sacramento with a saxophonist, a fellow by the name of Mike Butera, who I knew had become a Christian. I told Mike that I was grateful he called me for the gig and that I'd been praying for work and trying to get my life in order. He looked at me kind of weird. I wanted to tell him that because I wanted him to think that I was sort of "in the club."

About a month after that he called me and said, "First, I want to apologize for something that you don't even know about. I'm a Christian and I feel that ever since you came and played that gig with me, God has been impressing upon my heart that I should call you and see if I can come over and pray with you. I have been really embarrassed to do that and afraid that you would put me down." I remember just thinking, "Yeah, yeah, come on over." So he came over and we got to talking, and he really just explained the Gospel to me in a way that I had never heard before.

This time when I heard about sin, I knew exactly what he was talking about. When he spoke about being imperfect in light of a perfect God, I knew what he was saying. When he asked me if I thought I needed a savior, I knew I did because my best efforts to save myself had failed miserably. Everything in the language of redemption that he spoke about rang true to my heart and mind. After explaining the Gospel to me, he asked if I wanted Christ to live in my heart, if I wanted to become a Christian, and I just burst out crying. I said I wanted that more than anything. He didn't have to convince me that I needed a savior. I mean, if anybody needs a savior I need one. I still need one. Though I've been a Christian for quite awhile, I need to be reminded of the Gospel every day. It's by grace through faith in Christ and not by works that I have been saved from sin and my due punishment, and that is extremely good news!

Through the years Charlie Peacock's talents as a Christian artist and music producer have brought him many accolades including back-to-back Dove awards for Producer of the Year. His leadership in the Christian arts community has inspired a generation of up-and-coming Christian artists. Today, along with his continuing musical pursuits as an artist, producer, and A&R director for re:think Records, Charlie is an author/teacher specializing in the interface of music, commerce, and Christianity.

For some, God's calling can take years to receive. For others, it comes dramatically, in a moment, as it did for Lisa Bevill. With the calling also comes purpose.

Lisa Bevill

We all need to find out who we are. We need to find out how Christ created us and be who we're supposed to be instead of competing with one another. A lot of times in our industry there is a whole competitive thing set up, pressure is brought to bear on us to outperform and compete against other artists, and it's not right.

For the two years between the release of my first and second albums, I just had to keep remembering what it was like for me sitting on my couch at midnight and hearing the Lord talk to me and tell me, "*You are going to sing Christian music whether you like it or not, and this is what I intend for you to do!*" I had to keep remembering, "Okay, my calling . . . my calling, the Lord placed a calling on my life." I had to keep going back to that one night. He didn't call me to compete with so-and-so, or to be better than so-and-so, or to have a number one hit on the charts or win a Dove award. It's not about that. That's just taking credit for a gift and a talent that we really have nothing to do with. We're all meant to sing for one purpose and one purpose only: to save lives and to share Christ. There's no other reason than that.

Carolyn Arends remembers riding around with her "really cool family" picking out vocal harmonies from Gaither eight tracks. The following story illustrates how we are shaped by experiences with our families.

Carolyn Arends

I live in Vancouver, British Columbia, Canada. I had the *great fortune* of being born into a really cool family. I'm still really close to my mom and dad; in fact, they live about two blocks from where my husband and I live right now. I still rehearse in their basement, as do my other two brothers. It's been a long-term relationship with them.

I am the oldest, and I have two younger brothers. I grew up in a home that had a lot of laughter, and a lot of music, and a very real faith and love for God. I was pretty blessed in terms of how I started out. My parents were really into Christian music. It took me a long time to find out about other kinds of music. There was a time when I thought The Gaithers were the hippest thing going.

Crystal Lewis's family heritage illustrates that when your father is a minister and your mother is a "great musician," you stand poised to inherit the basic building blocks for a life in Gospel music.

Crystal Lewis

My father was a minister in Anaheim, California, for about seventeen years. I think he started there when I was about 2 or 3 years old. My dad pastored that church until I was 19 years old. Then he moved away to take another church elsewhere, and I remained. I got married and have been in southern California ever since.

I started singing early on, probably when I was about 4 or 5, in my dad's church. My mom is a great musician—an incredible pianist and a wonderful singer and songwriter as well. She accompanied me for years and years; she still does when I get to be with them in their church. So that's kind of how I started initially, just getting introduced to music and singing, and all of that was through my parents.

Then when I was about 15, I auditioned for the musical *Hightops* and I was in that, recorded an album, and did a little bit of live shows with them. Then I got into a band called Wild Blue Yonder. And when the band dismantled about a year and a half after we were signed to

Frontline, they allowed me to go on and do some solo projects. So that's how it all started.

One of the hardest lessons to learn is that of waiting on the Lord. The forming of the group Sierra is an object lesson in patience, trust, and faithfulness.

Sierra
(Wendy Foy Green, Deborah Schnelle, Jennifer Hendrix)

Wendy: I was living in Austin, Texas, where I was developing a solo artist ministry. My record label at the time hired a guy named Brian Green to produce my record. Brian had a bandmate named Rex Schnelle and while we were in the studio recording my album, we needed someone to help out with some of the background vocals. Rex knew a singer named Deborah and so we invited her to sing on the album. We noticed right away that when we sang separately, we sounded different. But when we sang together we blended so well that no one could tell us apart!

We laughed about that at the time, but what is really funny is that I ended up marrying Brian, and Deborah married Rex. Later they moved to Nashville, and I moved to Houston.

When I was living in Houston, I began seriously thinking about what I wanted to do with ministry and music. I decided that I had grown up with harmonies and that's what I really loved to do. I wanted to get a trio together, sing harmony, and minister as a group. The first person I thought of was Deborah. So I called her up in Nashville to see what she'd think about this.

Deborah: I answered the phone, and she said, "What do you think about this idea?" I said, "Wendy, this is what

I've been praying for." I had wanted to do music since arriving in Nashville, but I really felt God's call to wait upon Him and not to go chasing after things just to please myself. In order to be in the ministry it had to really and truly be from God or it would be all vanity. People would come up and encourage me to try to break in to the industry, but I just thought, *You know what, I'm just not interested in doing that.* God is literally going to have to drop it on my lap, and I will know without a shadow of a doubt it's from Him. So when I got that call I just knew, and I said, "Yes."

Wendy: And she asked who the third person was going to be. I said, "Well, my husband is producing a custom record for a really cute girl named Jennifer Hendrix. She sings great, so I'm going to give her a call and see what she says." So I called Jennifer in Lampassas, Texas.

Jennifer: I loved the sound of vocal trios and the idea of being in a group really intrigued me. So I told her, "Let me pray about this," and I got off the phone. But when I hung up the phone I yelled, "Mom, Dad, you won't believe what she just asked me!" And my dad said, "She wants you in the trio."(The week before Brian had told me and my dad about Wendy wanting to put together a trio.) I said, "I told her I'd pray about this, but I want to say yes!" I think I held out for 24 hours before I told her. I knew it was God.

Wendy: I was in Houston, Deborah was in Nashville, and Jennifer was in Lampassas. We had never sung together as a trio, so I asked them to come to Houston to record a three-song demo. We met in the studio and had parts for everyone. And as soon as we started singing together, we knew it was meant to be. The blend was something that only God could put together. It sounded like we were real sisters. So we finished that three-song demo, and Brian and I knew in our hearts that we were moving to Nashville. That is odd because up to that point moving to Nashville was the last thing that we wanted to do. It was an inside joke, but God changed our hearts and soon we found ourselves there. I asked Jennifer how fast she could get to town, and three weeks later, she arrived too, and we were all three in Nashville.

We sang for two years locally in and around Nashville under the name "By Design" before we ever really talked to anybody about a record deal. People would hear us at church and by word of mouth ask us what we wanted to do. Eventually we were signed by Star Song and became Sierra.

The call has come. Before long the artists will be asked to tell and retell their testimonies, to share their hearts about the God they have been called to serve.

2
I'M NOT ASHAMED

> "There are chapters in every life which are seldom read and certainly not aloud."
>
> Carol Shields, The Stone Diaries

FEW THINGS ARE CAPABLE of inducing more fear in the hearts of Christians than the thought of sharing their personal salvation testimony. Like public speaking, death, and dentistry, there are some things we would all just rather avoid.

If you grew up attending a Christian church, you may have at some time been entreated to write out the account of how and when you asked Christ into your heart. You may have even stood up at a summer youth retreat and nervously recited your story to other teens around the campfire, with your knees like jello and your nose filled with the smell of bug spray.

Surely these experiences, however awkward, were meant to challenge us to verbalize our faith. They helped make profound experiences more real and tested our mettle . . . but was it just kid stuff? Now you're an adult (or at least a little older and wiser) and it's time to take a fresh look at this testimony business and see what all the fuss is about.

What do you say to the idea of stepping back and reexamining your story one more time? What's the point? Well, just that this story of yours may be the most gripping and exciting aspect about you.

Telling it may be a doorway into deeper relationships with others, the kickoff to life-changing conversations, or a catalyst for conversion, connection, and being real. It may be the one facet that others in your life are dying for you to show them.

Why is that? Life comes to many of us with little or no instructions. We are all born to *"figure it out as we go along."* Saying that we are preoccupied with the lives of those around us is an enormous understatement. We are a society of voyeurs ever watchful to the activities of those across the street and behind the windows of the richest and poorest homes in town. Our cultural fascination with celebrities alone borders on mass addiction. We desperately desire to know what's going on inside the walls where other people live. Sometimes you and I are the people whom other people are watching.

Stories told about the events in others' lives have the ability to tune us in faster than a Beach Boys song on an oldies station. Stories about experiences that we ourselves have not had compel us. Your cosmic rendezvous with the God of the universe, to those who have not met Him, is just such a story. Often salvation testimonies are spiced up with enigmatic details such as mysterious strangers who "felt led to call you" just as you were praying to God for help or a letter with cash arriving on the day you're short on rent! God's authentic signature is on His work. We are His work and His body, and we need to be telling what we know.

So as you cruise through this chapter on personal testimony, watch for revelations. The people in this chapter will claim to have an ongoing relationship with a man who is known to have died 2,000 years ago! They will say that a Being capable of breathing creation into existence is interested in our puny lives. Their testimonies, Holy Ghost stories, may create in you a sense that the seldom read chapters of our lives are in fact the most vibrant and interesting. You may experience an irresistible urge to tell someone your own story. So draw the shades and dim the lights. . . . You may be touched by an unseen hand.

Newsong

(Eddie Carswell, Billy Goodwin, Leonard Ahlstrom, Scotty Wilbanks, Russ Lee)

Russ Lee: I've been a Christian for seventeen years. It's been the greatest seventeen years of my life. I gave my heart to Jesus back in 1980. My only regret since that time is that I didn't give my heart to Jesus sooner. I thank the Lord today that at 18 years of age, I prayed a simple prayer. No one was with me. It was late at night, and I was driving home by myself. I said, "God, I don't even know if You're up there. I don't know if You're real, but if You are and You can change this heart—or do anything with me—or You can make this life make sense, I'll do anything that You want me to do. Anything You show me that's true, I'll follow You. I just don't want to get to the end of my time here on earth whether I'm 18 or 80, and look back and find out that I missed the whole point of why I'm here and what life is about."

I prayed that prayer in silence, and I went home and cried myself to sleep that night, knowing that I was empty and desperately in need of some help from somewhere. I wasn't sure who God was or what He wanted to bring into my life or even if He was real. But for the next two nights I thought about that when I'd try to go to bed. Thursday night, Friday night . . . I was desperate.

In that moment of desperation, alone, I asked Jesus; I asked the Lord whoever He was to show me what was real, and what was right, and what I needed to do.

Two days later an old friend of mine knocked on the door. I hadn't seen him in years, and he told me that he had almost prayed the same thing, the same night after he had dropped his girlfriend off.

He had stopped at a little church where some of the kids in the area, including myself, used to go to Vacation

Bible School. He talked to the pastor, and the pastor told him about Jesus. He had given his heart to the Lord on a Thursday night and he came to tell me that he was going to be baptized on Sunday and to invite me to go to church with him. That was pretty odd because I lived way out in the country. Nobody ever came to see me just passing through, and I'd never known anybody to drive that far just to tell somebody that they needed to go to church. But he invited me to go to church with him, and I went to church that Sunday. The pastor told me that day about the love of Jesus, what He had done, how He had conquered death, hell, sin, and the grave for me. And how my sin was separating me from God. And you know what? I knew that. I knew that I was separated from God. I knew that I was a sinner. The evidence was strong; everybody knew that I was a sinner. But I knew that day that I could find what I was looking for in a personal relationship with Jesus Christ—because of what the pastor said, because of the love that I felt at that little church, and because of the reality and truth of the message.

Maybe you're reading this book, and you realize that there's something missing in your life. You've been looking a long time and maybe you've heard about Jesus, but you've never invited Him into your heart. I would encourage you to listen to the great messages of these songs and to the hearts of these men who have written and performed them. I would encourage you to realize that the thing that's different about their lives is who Jesus Christ is and what He's done for them. I want to remind you today that He doesn't love anybody more than He loves you—not even Billy Graham! He loves you, Jesus died for you, and He wants to change your life. More than dying for you, Jesus rose again and when He did, He's given us life abundant here on earth. He's also given us a promise of forever with Him. I believe that. For me, it started seventeen years ago, and it keeps getting better and better. Heaven is just too good to miss. I don't want you to miss it.

My prayer for you today is that you'll open your heart, surrender your life, and let Jesus Christ come in and change you. You'll be glad you did. It's the greatest decision a man or woman could make.

Our testimonies are not just our encounter stories. They are also the ongoing news of how Christ meets us every day. In Cindy Morgan's story, she tells where her heart was when she accepted Christ and how that shapes her thinking about ministry today.

Cindy Morgan

My mom and dad were such great Christians. I remember that I was about 5 or 6 when I first went up to the altar at the First Baptist of Harrogate and made my public dedication. But even then it was just to confirm to everyone else what I already knew in my heart.

Since then there have certainly been times when I've been closer to God. I feel closer to God now than I ever have. Looking back at the last several years I realize that I maybe didn't know Him that well at all. I knew the reputation and the image of Him, but it's been in the last several years that He's really become real to me.

There's a definite responsibility for a Christian artist, but whether you take that on is up to you. You can go into this and it can mean several things to you: It can mean, "Oh my dream is coming true, I'm getting to do what I've always wanted to do." Or it can mean, "I get to be a part of something that means people's lives will be changed for an eternity." Hopefully, in this business, it's about the latter. Otherwise your dream is going to be shattered really quickly because the struggle to believe that it's you is one that tears you apart. When you think, *Wow, I'm a great singer!* or *Wow, I have the best personality*, or *People are going to really want to know me*, you're kidding yourself, because who I am inside is bad—who I am, who I was born. I will be a bad person. I will think of myself. I will try to do things that make me look good. And the only thing in us that makes us do anything good and do anything worthwhile is Christ. It's Christ in us. Christ living in us—knowing Him, walking with Him. He is what makes us do good things.

I have been learning that you go up on that stage and on nights when it's good and on nights when it's bad, you should walk off equally happy that you have walked off with the same salvation that you walked on with.

The words in songs spring forth from the hearts of the writers. This testimony from Larnelle Harris speaks of the wellspring from which his music streams.

Larnelle Harris

We glorify this cross to the point that we think it wasn't such a big deal. We talk about it in terms of it being just some little happening, when in fact, this was the most cruel, the most inhumane way to be put to death. When we begin to think of what that was really like, that those nails were *real* spikes through *real* honest-to-goodness flesh, it was real bleeding and torture. I don't think we know what that's about enough to grasp that concept today, because we really don't understand what God's love is all about yet. The fact is that He really cares for us.

I wrote a song called "I Don't Know Why You Love Me" because that's true in my own life. Songs that I've written like "He Loved Me with a Cross" and others are written and recorded because I'm still trying to understand what that was about. How could someone love someone so much that He would go to the cross and die for them? I understand that it should have been me on the cross, my good friends, my wife and kids. But it wasn't. It was Jesus Himself, God in the flesh. That breaks my heart. I'm still trying to understand that, and I'm certain that I'm not the only one.

I want to sing about the cross. Do you know why? Because it is at that crossroad that people must decide. It is in the light of the cross that mankind must decide which direction to go. It is at that juncture that John 3:16 begins to make any sense to us: *"For God so loved the world that He gave His only begotten Son, that whoever believes in Him should not perish, but have everlasting life."*

When I go out to have a concert or any artist that you interview, the promoters will advertise, "Larnelle, Larnelle is coming!" That's okay at the beginning. But when I leave, I don't want them saying, "Larnelle," anymore; I want them saying, "Jesus, Jesus, Jesus," because He's the only thing that can make a difference in a life. The reckoning with that kind of love totally breaks your heart.

When I think about it, big tears roll down my face because it *totally breaks my heart* to think that someone loved me that much. Why do I want to sing about it? Because that's the only song, the only lyric, the only thought. Every song that we sing has to go back to that.

Every insight the late Rich Mullins ever gave seemed to be based on his own real-life experience. I never met Rich Mullins in person. Once, when he was at the radio station KLTY in Dallas, and I was in Nashville, we spoke over the phone for almost an hour. I can't remember a single answer that wasn't soaked with the reality of Jesus.

Rich Mullins

Maybe more than ever before twentieth-century people live without any identity. They live without any sense of being anything other than something with needs and wants. We define ourselves in terms of our sexual preference. We define ourselves in terms of recreational preferences. We talk about ourselves in those kinds of terms. I think it's because we largely live on sensation. We rarely get beyond sensation into anything that's essential. I think it's because we're afraid that if we ever get past this little shallow thing that we're playing out that we're going to find out there's nothing under it. I find that what parades itself as piety often is nothing but pure doubt. That it's really agnosticism dressed up in a lot of religious jargon.

So for me, I think it would be really easy to say, "I think what would really please God is if I don't dance, I don't chew, and I don't go with girls who do." It would be easy to say, "Oh, gee, I think what will really please God is if I become an evangelist and convert a thousand people." It's much more difficult I think for me to become who I am and who He created me to be because no one else can tell me when I've accomplished that. But that's one of the things I find beautiful in the book of Revelation is when Jesus says, *"To him who overcomes I will give a white stone and on that stone is a name known only to the person who receives it and to me."* The white stone signifies victory and could very well hint at purity. Jesus said only the pure heart will see God. I would love to hear that in a sermon sometime instead of being asked to come forward. I would love to hear a pastor say, "If you want to see God then make your heart pure."

The significant thing to me is there is a name on that stone that is the name Jesus knows me by. My mother does not know me by that name. My friends don't know me by that name. No one in this world, including myself, knows who I really am. I think that when we see ourselves in light of Jesus, which will only happen when we give up ourselves and begin to seek Him wholeheartedly, then we will eventually grow into the person that He meant for us to be. When we see our name on that stone we'll say, "Wow, that's me! How did You know me when I couldn't even know myself?" For me, that's part of the goal of spiritual maturity.

We'd like to be able to tell everyone about the love and forgiveness we've experienced as Christians and have them fall to their knees experiencing the same forgiveness. It doesn't always happen just like that way. With the help of his pastor, Michael O'Brien may have found a way of telling his story when words get in the way.

Michael O'Brien

My pastor at Newsong Christian Fellowship has really inspired me to be a man of conviction, to truly live what I believe, to make sure that the lyrics of each song point to the hope that we as Christians have. The whole concept behind the album *Conviction* came from me wanting to be a man my children could look up to. If there is anything worthwhile I could ever give them, it would have to be a life of service. Christ is the center of all that. I want to stand up for Him in all aspects of what I do. I'm not the example . . . Jesus is. But I believe God is calling me to reach out to the multitudes, to let them know I am a Christian, and then let my life be an example.

My father is not a believer. I classify him as the Archie Bunker/Al Bundy of my life. We would get together and would always get in arguments about religion and he would tell me how if he were God, how he would have done things differently. He can't believe in something he can't see. But I believe the Spirit of God gave me the wisdom on how to deal with him. There's a time to talk and there's a time to be quiet and live it. So, I wrote a song ("If I Said Nothin'") which fits into this whole concept.

My Dad, of course, doesn't like it because it reminds him that we are on two different paths. So I have to watch what I am saying in concert if he is around, even though he knows it was written for him. But I have found that reaching out to him in love and serving him is breaking him. He doesn't understand why I want to take care of him as he gets older. Then I tell him that the Lord put him on my heart. He smiles. There are other people in our lives we come in contact with that we may not be sure how to share the gospel with. God's Spirit will show us how we should approach each individual. The one thing that separates us from the world is our hope in the Cross: We realize we can't live without it and they don't see their need of it. My prayer for my dad and others is that they will see their need for a Savior and make the decision that will ultimately change their lives forever.

I asked Michael Card what his ambitions were when he first started in Christian music. Since Michael is frequently referred to as one of the best practitioners of Christian artistry, it's interesting to think of him as ever having a growth curve.

Michael Card

I've been doing this for fifteen years now. When I first started, I know I took myself more seriously than I do now. I think I took what I did more seriously in the wrong sense. I wanted to be able to create a body of work that would be helpful, to help people work through the Bible. I think I based too much importance on my own self in that whole process. Now, I think it's right in thinking how things gradually get stripped away [in the Christian walk]. My consistent prayer now has been reduced to: *"Lord, let me be Your man."* Before, when we'd play in concert I used to have a whole series of things that I would pray every night to try to focus in. Now, I guess out of desperation more than anything else, my prayer and my desire are: *I just want to be the Lord's man.* Whatever that means, because it means a whole wealth of things. But that's what it's been reduced to for me.

Some in the Church have worked overtime to prove that you can be Christian *and cool.* Crystal Lewis learned that going to church is a privilege and a lot of fun.

Crystal Lewis

We were taught early on that [going to church] was a privilege. I remember my father overhearing me talk over the phone to a friend who asked me to go somewhere over the weekend. And it didn't happen just once, you know, it was something that happened often: Your friends ask you to do something on the weekend and they don't go to church. A lot of my school friends didn't, so they'd want me to come spend the night on Saturday night, mess around on Sunday, and I would say, "No, I have to go to church." Dad would always say, "You know what, you don't *have to* go; you get to go. It's a privilege in this country to have the freedom to worship the way that we do."

I was taught early on that it was a privilege to be there when the doors were open. And fortunately for me, my group of friends was my youth group. Those were the people I hung out with. I was very involved with school and that sort of thing and I was always very eager to be there at church on Sunday. Whatever the youth group activities were, that was exciting to me.

It was an extremely normal parent-child relationship as far as butting heads, and arguing, and all of that sort of thing as well. Though I enjoyed my church group and that was in fact my group of friends, I most definitely had my share of rebellious teenage moments. They weren't overboard, thank God, but I was a brat. My dad's favorite word for me was *belligerent*. I was extremely strong-willed and had a mind of my own, and so did they, so it caused a lot of butting heads. But it also caused a lot of structure that was good and that I learned from. All in all, I wouldn't trade it for the world.

We all have set ideas about what things are really like, and church is just one of those things that have been clichéd. I like this story in particular that Rick Cua tells about what turned the light on for him about church: seeing God's love in action in people at the church.

Rick Cua

I would go to church day in and day out; it was a routine for me. I can remember going to the Catholic church in my neighborhood and all the men stood at the back and as soon as Communion was over we were out the door. We just went there. We felt good because we went, and I'm sure that on occasion there were things that happened within the church that inspired us, but basically I didn't have that personal relationship.

After my wife got saved, I saw her living out the life of a Christian a little more. She was more serious about serving

God and about reading the Bible, being in prayer, and being a helper to other people. When she would take me to church with her, which was as often as I wanted to go, I saw all different types of people loving one another: who I call the "cool" people and the "nerdy" people, the musician types and the businessmen, the blue-collar workers; I saw everybody—all different types truly in fellowship and loving one another. I realized although I loved people, I didn't have quite that. I loved *my group, my gang,* the people that I thought were birds of a feather, so to speak. But I saw such a wonderful fellowship within the church, and I knew it was because these people first loved God. The love of God was in them and I wanted that.

I wanted it more than anything. I wanted to be a good man, a godly man. I mean a good man not just in deed, but I wanted to be a man of God. At that point, because I think that desire came over me, the Lord revealed Himself to me in a real way and I got saved.

There's more than one way to share the hope that you have. Actions speak louder than words. Gary Chapman shares not only how he makes his faith visible, but he also points out who is watching.

Gary Chapman

I've always been kind of a late bloomer. I just turned 40, and that's kind of late to be starting, but I really feel like I am. I feel like all the things I've done over the past twenty years in this town have prepared me for the stuff I'm doing now, and that's just God's timing. He does with us what He wants to do, once we tell Him that's okay with us, and I said that a long time ago. I've got a lot to be thankful for. I love my jobs and I have several of them. I'm thankful for an opportunity to be a public Christian. I'm not ever going to slam anybody over the head with a Bible. I'm pretty low-key about it, but extremely unashamed at the same time. I think that God uses the fact that I'm willing to be completely open with my Christianity to put me in places that He might not want somebody who might judge folks or come down hard or preach at them or whatever. I hope He's honored by that.

On the more personal level, my family is everything to me. It's what everything revolves around. It's what matters. I obviously want to please God with what I'm doing, but the work ethic and commitment level and the ability to try, fail, or succeed—all those things I'm trying to live out in my life I'm doing for my kids. I want them to see that and learn. I want them to see me disappointed and how I deal with that. I want them to see me elated and how I deal with it. I want them to see the whole gamut of life experience and have some foundation for attacking it on their own because it will happen before I can turn around. I can't believe they are as old as they are. I feel the compelling need and simultaneously the call to live life fully in front of them. That's what really drives me more than anything else.

I am who I am, and I am unashamedly a Christian. The fact that I'm getting an opportunity to be on a secular show is a great opportunity, and it's a gift. When it's right I talk about it. I really believe the "us" and "them" mentality that we've created (sorry, we're responsible) during the past twenty years or so and the judgment that we've brought into the lives of Americans in terms of what they think of when they think [negatively], *Wow, a Christian* is damaging. I hate that, and I'm going to do everything I can to dismantle it. I do that by being exactly who I am and being completely unashamed of my faith, but never, ever judging anyone. That's hard to do because it's a natural tendency.

God has a perfect plan for our lives. In a few short paragraphs, Morgan Cryar tells of finding it through his change from heartsick teenager to aspiring college grad.

Morgan Cryar

As I was getting out of my junior year and into my senior year in high school it started to occur to me that there was something to this [Christianity]. I was starting to think that there had to be more than just going to church every Sunday and just sitting through this. There's got to be something going on.

During my senior year I fell deeply in love with this girl across the state line in Texas. After some time she jilted me. She told me she didn't love me anymore. It was so deep of an experience to be rejected. I had given my heart over to her, which was foolish. That devastation literally drove me to my knees where I said, *"Lord, if I am such an unstable person who destroys my life this much, I have to find You. I have to really, truly root myself into You."* I sought God really for the first time in my life. I had been baptized as a kid and done the church membership thing in the Baptist church were I grew up. But it was a more committed thing that happened then. I threw myself at God and said, *"I will have no more of myself, I want You."* It was like a ravenous hunger. I had to have God.

I sensed that there was a call that was to be on my life. This wasn't going to be a fad. I sensed that God *really* wanted to do something with me. At that point, all I knew was that if God called you, He must be calling you to preach. So I went to college and studied to become a pastor. This happened right at the end of high school, so I went straight for it. I had no doubts about that until I started writing music. I had played music all my life, but it was always something just for fun.

It had never occurred to me that someone like me could go out there and do that. Then I met some guys in college who wrote music, and I thought, *If they can do this, I can at least try.*

Before I got out of college I realized that this could be what God wanted me to do, so I began to take it seriously. I set my mind to it, sent out demos, and got a lot of refusals before I eventually got some positive response.

This interview with Scott Wesley Brown was one of the first I'd ever done. He shared this story of an unusual way of finding the Lord.

Scott Wesley Brown

I'll never forget that I went to the pastor of our church when I was growing up and I said, "Tell me, what is the difference between Jesus and Mohammed and Buddha and all these other guys? Can I believe in all of them or should I just pick one and kind of go for it? Is Jesus the only way?" And I'll never forget what he said to me; he said, "You know, Scott, you just need to follow your heart and be true to yourself and wherever you end up, it's okay." I'm glad he said that. Because even though it was totally ridiculous, it made me *so mad* that he was a Christian minister and he denied Jesus. It angered me and something in that statement made me think, *I'd better check out Jesus.* I don't know why that statement disturbed me so much, maybe it was the hypocrisy of him being a Christian pastor and then giving me this universalist kind of a statement. That really made me start looking at Jesus.

Because I was so angered at this statement, I went to a friend who was a Christian and I told him that the pastor told me, "Hey, whatever your heart wants to follow, truth is relative." My friend said, "No, you've got to really look at Jesus." I said, "Yeah, but there's so much hypocrisy in the Church and this pastor's so hypocritical." I'll never forget what my friend said. He said, "You're right. There is a lot of hypocrisy in the church. Christians aren't perfect, and they're going to make mistakes. There are others who say they're Christians, but they really aren't. But don't look at them; look at Jesus. Really look at Jesus and who He said He was, and you'll realize that He is everything that He said He was." And I did.

I started looking at Jesus.

I got involved in a band that was leading worship at some revivals at a local church where I was living. They needed a guitar player, so I filled in although I wasn't a believer. I went through the whole summer right before my senior year in high school playing in this Christian music group, leading worship even though I didn't even believe yet, but I was attracted! I saw this warmth and this genuineness in a lot of the lives of the people. The more I looked at Jesus, the more I wanted to know Him, but I was really afraid to make that commitment.

Our youth group went on a retreat at the end of the summer down to Virginia Beach. While we were there I just happened to stumble onto this Christian coffee-house. I went into this coffeehouse, and there was a band playing Christian music. You've got to realize this was back in 1970, and there was hardly anything happening in Christian music back in 1970. This band was so good, and I was in this room with all these neat little Christian posters up about love and peace. It felt like it was more than just words that I'd heard down in the streets of Washington, D.C., where all the hippies were marching for peace at the time. People were really genuinely loving me and being kind to me. I felt this unbelievable atmosphere of love. It was all centered around Jesus, and I wanted it so much.

I went up to the manager of this coffeehouse and I said, "Listen, I do some Christian music. If you ever need someone to fill in, I'd love to do it." He said, "Hey, tomorrow night the band is off. How about you coming over here and let me audition you before we open? If it works, we'll put you on."

So I went back and told the youth group that they might let me play, so let's all go down there. So the next night, we got there early. I was on the back steps of this coffeehouse and the guy came out. I sang a couple of these songs that I'd learned in this worship band at the revival meetings. He said, "Hey, it sounds good. Why don't you go on up and minister?" So I got up there on the stage, and I did my first Christian set—*and I'm not a Christian at this point.* I'm doing my very first Christian concert and at the end of the first set I give this invitation and people in my youth group give their lives to Christ. I thought, *Hey, this is really cool.* I sat at one of the tables and I was having a Coca-Cola or something, and the manager came over and said, "Brother, praise the Lord! That was just absolutely fantastic! You have a real gift for this. How long have you been a Christian?" I looked at him and I said, "Well, ah . . . I'm not a Christian." And he said, "What ?" I said, "I'm not a Christian." He said, "What do you mean *you're not a Christian?* You were just up there telling everyone they had to give their lives to Jesus, and you're not a Christian?" So I shared some of my struggle with him, and he said, "Man why don't you go up there the next set and tell everyone what you just told me. Why don't you give your life to Christ?" I thought, *Oh, I can't go up there in front of all these people after I've invited them to come to Christ and tell them, "Hey, well, I'm not a Christian, but I'm going to become one right now and before your very eyes.*" And I chickened out. I got up there and just sang a bunch of the worship songs I knew, prayed a little prayer, and then left.

I remember I went back to this house that our youth group had rented for the week or two that we were down at the beach. I remember going back and putting my guitar away and then walking out onto the beach in front of the ocean. It was probably around 11:30 at night, and it was a beautiful moon. It was just one of those gorgeous nights at the beach. And I remember I just started to cry and I said, "God, *I really want to know You.* I just want to know You more than anything else. You're the most important thing in my life and You're the most important thing in all of life. I really have a lot of questions, and I've still got doubts. I'm still confused, but I just know there's something about Your Son, Jesus, and I want Him to come into my life." I prayed the same prayer that I'd heard them praying all summer in this revival meeting, because I knew it by memory, and I invited Jesus to come into my heart.

Then I guess I thought a band of angels was going to come down and play some song! But it was just quiet. All I could hear was just the waves crashing in. But I did in my heart feel this peace. It wasn't some kind of a magical, mystical kind of peace. It was just a simple feeling that I had made a decision now to follow Jesus, to give my life to Him, and to call Him Lord.

I went across the street and there was another pastor who was on our youth group retreat with us that week. He was a believer, so I said, "I want you to know that I just gave my life to Christ." Eventually I was able to get involved in an organization called Young Life for the rest of high school and then later on InterVarsity in college where I was discipled. That made the big difference because then I began to get the biblical foundation for the decision that I'd made. That was some twenty-six years ago.

Does it matter where you come from or what you've done before you come to Christ? Kirk Franklin shares his important story on this issue.

Kirk Franklin

I was adopted when I was 4. I used to run and get in fights, smoke and drink, and go out. I was in the Church, but the Church wasn't in me. I had a friend get killed when I was 15, and I knew I needed to make some changes. I was raised dirt cheap, but it didn't stop me. I disagree with people who say they are the way they are because of their condition. I mean, I was raised bad, too, but I chose to go the other way. Anybody who thinks their circumstance will dictate their future, that devil is a lie, because it didn't happen to me.

When we decide to give God our lives, we may find ourselves in places we never expected, answering questions we never expected to hear. Ken Holloway once had this experience.

Ken Holloway

I was on *Music City Tonight* in September of '95. I got up and started singing "Hoedown." I got into the first couple of lines of the song and saw people out of the corner of my eye stumbling, trying to catch something. It was the hosts, Lorianne Crook and Aaron Tippin, fumbling through my CD cover, trying to read the words as I was singing. They just flipped over the song. When I got off and went over to the couch and did the interview, they just flipped over the music, flipped over the songs, and they said, "*We didn't know Christians could have that much fun!* We didn't know y'all rock that much." We went back and forth and talked.

They told me right before going on, "She'll ask you how many number one singles you've had, how many awards you've won, but the subject of you becoming a Christian will not be discussed tonight." I said, "That's fine, whatever. I'm just glad to be here." So she leaned back and said, "So, Ken, tell us what happened, what changed your life?" In front of seventy million homes, I got to share that I came in stone drunk one night and high on drugs and my wife rolled over in bed and prayed out loud, and that's what changed my life. Lorianne Crook was just sitting there with tears in her eyes looking at me like, *Oh my gosh, what did we get here?* When the camera was off and the show was over, she was just searching for my wife in the audience. She went out and grabbed my wife and was all over her. They just hit it off, and my wife got to share some things. She said, "Ken was a mess before he got saved and now he's just a different person."

We did that and it was just incredible! These people treated us great. Then we did the Wildhorse.

Katie Haas was backstage. She pulled me aside and said, "Hey, this 'Hoedown' song is a hit. I don't care what they call it. I don't care if it's a Christian song, Country song, I don't care what they call it." She said, "So is this the theme? Is this what you feel heaven is going to be like?" I said, "Yeah." She said, "I don't remember a song this cool before ever in my life in Country music." And we're live on the air taping. And she said, "So, Ken, let's get to the nitty-gritty here. You were coming in drunk, you were having problems doing this and that, what happened?" Then again in front of all these millions of people, I got to share my testimony.

I sang at Fan Fair with Faith Hill and Lari White on the show. It was incredible. I got on stage and the people knew who I was. I started singing and some people were saying, "Wow! This guy sounds like a Country singer. What is he doing saved?" They were coming backstage saying, "Why are you still doing Christian music? It doesn't make any sense! Why don't you just go out and do Country and get mega-rich?" There again, I got to share some more. So, they're opening up in a major way.

The passion on our hearts is sharing the message that life is found only in Christ. We tell our stories, and we tell His. We embrace people who need this message of love, forgiveness, and acceptance through Jesus Christ. Let's take a look at the message.

3 THE MESSAGE

"'Love the LORD your God with all your heart, with all your soul, and with all your mind.' . . . 'Love your neighbor as yourself.'"

Jesus Christ, Matthew 22:37, 39

THE TRAIL GOES SOMETHING LIKE THIS: A writer in Nashville is inspired to write a piece of music that God has placed in his heart. The song is later recorded by an artist who selects it because he, too, finds it resonates in his spirit. The radio station in your town feels that it fits in well with their ministry to you and that it's the kind of song you'd like to hear. And you hear it while driving home from work one night and its message again strikes a chord, this time within you.

But here's where it gets really interesting. On the other side of the country, far removed from Music City USA, you've got your own problems. Perhaps your marriage isn't doing so great, or you are single and wish you had a partner, you need money to pay bills, or a loved one is ill, or you've just lost a job. Shall I go on? That message, crafted in the music, reminds us of God's eternal love for us. It reminds us of the truth that we are beloved children of God, and we are strengthened by it. We are made stronger by a message woven into a song, written by someone we'll never know, and sung by another whom we may never meet. The message, however, is recognized and welcomed. It reaches us at a time when we are receptive to what it uniquely brings.

The difference between Christian music and other forms of music is that Christian music is saturated with the Spirit of God. People are touched and ministered to by other forms of music, but none are brought closer to their Maker through listening, because none of those songs contain the name of Jesus, His promises, or His message.

This chapter examines the beliefs of many different contemporary Christian artists. Artists talk candidly about their motivations and goals for their ministerial vocations. This foundation allows us to begin understanding where the songs come from, what's happening on the concert trail, and why listeners are being spiritually moved by the message.

Michael W. Smith

"Live the Life" is probably my favorite and the most important song on the album *Live the Life* because it's how I really believe we can affect the world for Christ. I've always felt like we talk too much. There's been a lot of double-standard living and a lot of hypocrisy. Based on my experiences in the mainstream world I'd say: People don't want to hear it—they want to see it. When they see it, then they start inquiring about it, which is what they did with me.

When you can have an effect that way, when you're not beating someone over the head with a Bible, when you have someone look at you and say, "*There's something different about you. I want to know what it is,*" then you've hit a triple. You're potentially ready to walk across home plate in terms of sharing the gospel with people. I've been preaching "live the life" for a long time. It's just that now it manifested itself into a song.

Living the Christian life in front of others is one message we need to hear. Another is the importance of loving God with all our hears, following Him, and loving our neighbors as ourselves.

4 HIM

(Marty Magehee, Kirk Sullivan, Andy Chrisman, Mark Harris)

I think the one thing that drew us to that title [*The Message*] is the fact that that's what we're all about. The ministry of 4 HIM has always been about *the message* and about making sure people knew where we stood. I think that our message is just that *Jesus Christ is the Lord and Savior of our lives,* and hopefully when you look at 4 HIM on stage or hear our music we portray that.

Hopefully, our music and our stage performances will draw people closer to the Lord. Maybe they'll see in us something that they want—the love that we have for our Lord and Savior and the love that we have for one another. I think that the message is very simple: It's *to love God with all your heart* and *to follow Him* and then *to love people.* Love your neighbor as yourself.

Rich Mullins died in September 1997. The following interview took place with Rich a year earlier. Mostly we talked about what Rich believed. He had moved to the Southwest to teach music to Navajo children on a reservation. He spoke candidly about his own spiritual life.

Rich Mullins

Part of my motivation for moving out to the reservation, quite honestly, was that I had become very weary of twentieth-century American evangelical Christianity. I think it's okay. I don't have anything against it. I just don't think it's the whole picture. I think that putting yourself in a midst of a culture unlike the one you grew up in helps you to keep some sort of sense of balance in the way you view your faith, your life, and things going on around you.

I'm learning much more about being receptive to the work of God. I suppose I'm an evangelical. I think I'm sort of a lapsed evangelical or I used to flirt with it. I'm not sure what I've ever been if you really want to know the whole truth. There's this real unconscious sort of spiritual grooming going on all the time—not growing, just grooming. There's all that lingo that . . . "*anointed*" business. "Saved." "Anointed." "Blessed." It's cool to be around people who for no good reason have chosen a different lingo. So instead of saying, "That song was really anointed," they say, "That song really touched me." Which is I think the same thing that white middle-class Christians mean when they say "anointed." I'm not sure what they mean. My understanding of "anointed" in the Bible is they did it to people. The idea of a song being "anointed" is just really bizarre to me.

I think the one thing in my own spiritual life that's the most crippling to me is to become overly comfortable, to become overly familiar. To treat things that were holy as if they were not special. When you hear a person who has grown up being a shepherd talk about the Good Shepherd it brings this whole new side of the picture to me. It challenges the images that I contrived when I heard stories about the Good Shepherd. I think that most of the middle-class Christians are very sincere in their faith. I just think that for all of us, it's very easy to become very narrow.

I know that a lot of people think I'm this kind of liberal or something. I don't like the terms *liberal* and *conservative*.

I think I'm more conservative than most conservatives and more liberal than most liberals. I think if you ever met a good conservative or a good liberal, you'd probably like them very much. But it's hard to find a good one of either of those.

The thing that I generally do [to deal with the different understanding of God in the Navajo nation] is I listen respectfully—even though as a Christian I am a monotheist and have a system of theology that I've worked out for myself that is very different from the traditional Navajo religion. I still believe what marks us as Christians is not our doctrine in terms of a doctrinal statement. What marks us as Christians is our love for people. And if you love people you respect them. When someone who comes from a different religion, who comes from even a false religion, speaks, you listen respectfully to them. You know, I have a great mom. Once we were talking about a friend of ours who . . . it's just wild that she and my mom are friends. I asked, "Do you ever feel weird around her?" and my mom said, "Yeah, sure I do!" But here's the deal: No one was ever won into the kingdom of God through snobbery. We come to know Christ through love. I really believe that. I'll tell you the truth, I think that all these doctrinal statements that all the congregations come up with over the years are basically just not very worthwhile. I don't mean to sound mean toward the people who came up with them. I understand in the past there have been many heretical movements, and we still need to maintain sound doctrine in terms of a good understanding of how God works and operates. But I think our real doctrine is that doctrine that is born out in our character. I think you can profess the Apostles' Creed until Jesus returns, but if you don't love somebody you never were a Christian.

The gospel continues to move David Meece to passion. Forgiveness will always be a great reason to jump up and down in celebration.

David Meece

The most gratifying aspect of being a Christian is knowing that whatever we do today, whatever mistakes we make, are not necessarily things that are going to destroy us for the rest of our lives.

People are really good at remembering every little thing we do wrong. Jesus isn't like that. Our heavenly Father isn't like that. Christianity is not to be like that. I wrote the song "Once in a Lifetime." It's one of those few songs that I'll say in concert, *"You know, I like this song."* I like what it says: "No matter where we've been, no matter what we've done, today can be our once in a lifetime." When we ask the Lord Jesus into our heart and we ask God to forgive, He is faithful and just to forgive us. Period! That's it, it's over, it's gone, history, outta here. It didn't happen. It's gone, it's erased. I wish people could do that. People can't do that, God does that. That's the mighty power of the blood of Jesus, that it washes clean completely. "Yesterday is gone, tomorrow may not come. This moment is our once in a lifetime."

Right now, you and I, no matter what we've done in our lives (*this is mind-boggling*), we can get down on our knees and say, "Lord Jesus, come into my heart, forgive me of my sins, set me on a new place, let me begin again". . . and *you can!* Isn't that unbelievable? Where else can you do that? When you come before Him with a heart sincerely asking for forgiveness, He will forgive you, and you can start all over again. Your life can literally begin again, and you don't have to worry about one single thing that happened one moment before. To me, that's what Jesus on the cross is all about, and that is one of the things that excites me about going around and sharing the good news of Jesus Christ. You've got all these people walking around with all this baggage, all these hurts, all this stuff, saying, "I'm no good. I'm not good enough to go to church. I'm not good enough to be a Christian. I just can't do this," and it is a lie of Satan, my friend. You can say, "Jesus, Lord, forgive me right now," and He is faithful and just to do so. That's exciting.

Englishman Chris Eaton has recorded just three albums in the last fourteen years, but what terrific albums they've been. In between recording, he has written songs for Amy Grant, Russ Taff, Donna Summer, Cliff Richards, Patti Austin, and many others. The message Chris seems most interested in these days is obedience and its relationship to freedom.

Chris Eaton

There are certain rules that are made for a good reason. For example, you don't put your finger in a socket because it will electrocute you. As we grow up as Christians, we're always putting our finger in sockets because *we just want to see what it feels like to be electrocuted!* When we get electrocuted, we go back to God and go, "Why didn't you tell me not to put my finger in the socket?" We blame God for the things that go wrong in our lives when God's saying, "I told you in the first place, *you just didn't listen to me.*" We say we want to listen to Him, then we do our own thing. Why are Christians crying all the time because things aren't working out in their lives? Why are we living a non-healed life? I don't want to be glib about illness and why some things happen in our lives. I have no idea the answer to those questions, but I really believe in so many cases all of us can be lifted out of our mire, not becoming super-spiritual, but just enjoying God's life in us. Letting it go and letting Him deal with it. He wants to. He's got the plan. He's our Father. He loves us more than we'll ever know. So let Him do it. Let Him be in control and make the right choices. Do that and move on.

This album [*What Kind of Love*] is about discovering fun ways of being a Christian. The song "Shooting Stars" is all about the passions of life. It's not wrong to be passionate about things. It's not wrong to fly your kite and go, "*Oh, I love flying my kite!*" It's not wrong to be in love with someone *passionately* and to love them and to do crazy things with them within the right context. But just make sure you've got the rules of God that hold you around because He's just protecting you from falling off the cliff. If you're with the person that you're meant to be with, in the right rules that God has laid down in the Bible, then if you want to make love at the top of a mountain in the pouring rain, passionately, do it! It will be a wonderful thing—a wonderful memory that you can hold on to for the rest of your life. But if you're in a situation where God isn't granting the purpose for that, and it's not what He wants, you'll probably fall off the cliff and have to climb up all that way again.

What I'm just learning now is the pursuit of the right choices and making the wrong ones at the same time is not what God wants. Most of us are all wanting God's heart. We all want to see it in each other. We want to dispense with the pain and get on with just living and enjoying together. But that means making the right choices. For me, if I make the wrong choice or I'm holding on to something that deep down I know I should fix and I'm not fixing it, how can I expect God to change my feelings? How can I expect God to actually give me that joy if I'm not prepared to let Him deal with things? I long to get back to a balanced position of consistent Christian living in my life, where I'm not having to analyze myself all the time and think, "Did you really make the right choice that day?" I don't want to live like that! I want to live in freedom and joy and I know the key to that is doing what God tells me to do.

On their first album, Out of the Grey sang of wanting to see someone "on the other side of heaven's door." The song went on to say that that's the most important thing. I asked if there was a "most important thing" today in their music and ministry.

Out of the Grey
(Scott Dente, Christine Dente)

Christine: We always perform the song "Wishes" whenever we play, and it is still a common theme. Whether we're playing for an audience that we don't know or an audience of friends and family, we're always, ultimately, wishing that the simple gospel of Jesus comes across.

I think that's still our theme today. Our lives are a lot more complicated, we know a lot more people, we really have to struggle to be praying for those people, but we're still praying for them.

And ultimately, this life is but a sigh. It will be gone. So we better have a real legacy of a life lived in Christ or there's nothing. The music will fade away; there will be nothing.

Christine Dente speaks of what issues our lives should be about. Andrae Crouch gives us the reason artists are to sing, purified through thirty years of service.

Andrae Crouch

God first gave me the gift of music at age 11 and He gave me my first song at the age of 14. Now, as I think about the last thirty years, I don't even look at it as a career. I see it more as how God has directed my life and uniquely planned and woven it.

When I first gave my heart to the Lord, I was 9 years old. I had no idea that a career like this was in store for me then because, really, there was no one else I could pattern myself after.

I never knew then there would be a time when I would be on the road because I'd never heard of such a thing. I'd heard of missionaries that used to visit our church, but I'd never really heard of a singing missionary.

My father was a real lover of music. He allowed us to listen to a lot of different kinds of music. That in part shaped my style of music. Sometimes my parents would have these little taco parties at the house and my dad would ask me to sing something for some of his friends. In doing so, I always chose the songs that I thought that both the white people and the black people who were there could understand. That shaped my style too.

People began asking my sister and me and different ones that I was playing with to travel to different places and perform. But my dad would say, "It's not the time." My father was one to make sure that we didn't go out there prematurely. My parents made sure that we knew what we were singing about.

So we would sing on street corners; he would be preaching on Saturdays. And our church choir had a ministry to go in once a month to the prison here in southern California. I was 14 at the time when they allowed me to come in. I was supposed to be no younger than 18, but because I played for the choir, they allowed me to come in. So by the time I went out on the road I had already ministered on street corners, in hospitals, in prisons, and definitely at church. I knew what I was doing. I knew Scripture and my focus was in the right place to be out there to win souls for Jesus, not for a popularity contest.

One thing my father told me was, "If you're not out there to win souls, Andrae, you might as well pack up and come home, because your reason to do what you do is to win souls for Jesus Christ and that's it."

As time goes by, we learn to be exceedingly grateful for the things that we have. Thankfulness and how God changes our hearts over time. That's the message.

Wayne Watson

The older I get, the less there is to be proud of and the more there is to be thankful for. Most of my life I've been spiritually proud of things I haven't done wrong. You get to the place where you make little trophies for yourself. I'm more thankful for my family than I am proud of them, because I realize most of what they are is out of my hands. Most of what has happened to me in my career is not a result of me walking the streets of Nashville with songs trying to get them cut or trying to get a record deal. Most of it has been the blessing of God. So my "thankfulness" list is growing much longer and my "proud of" list is growing much shorter.

Christian artists sometimes start out with one set of ideas of how God will use them and end up with another. Glad shares their story of how God changed their hearts and minds.

Glad

(Chris Davis, Jim Bullard, Ed Nalle, John Gates, Paul Langford)

Ed: When we started out twenty some years ago, we thought we were going to be like a big secular rock band. Then we would tell everybody we were Christians, and they'd all fall down and worship the Lord. I think that's how every [Christian] band starts out, and of course it's ridiculous. Then we started to develop a style, and God started to work in our lives. We were all very immature Christians when we started the band. If fact, when we first started the band one of our members was not a Christian at all. But he was a *really great piano player* so I chose him anyway, which showed how mature I was. Then he accepted the Lord, and God began to work in our lives. Through the churches we were involved in and various teaching we heard along the way, we came to understand that we would have a ministry, not just be a band.

So when we got out of college we started to pursue a music ministry. We had no idea what that would mean and really no guideline to follow. There was no one around who could tell us how to do this, so we just stumbled along and kind of made it up as we went. *And God has been gracious.*

At the beginning we were young and stupid! We were young and we loved the music and none of us had wives or children. We just wanted to go out and try this, thinking we'd become famous and all of that kind of stuff. Over time, God took away the desire to be famous and replaced it with a desire to communicate with integrity and biblical accuracy.

Are artists in a contest just to win awards for themselves? Why are they doing what they do?

Cindy Morgan

We've got to remember it's not about approval. It's not about awards. I know that totally just sounds like the right thing to say, but it's so true that what we're doing is so much bigger than that. It's so much bigger than an award. I'm not knocking it, it's a nice thing, but I'm saying it's a trophy of sorts. But it reminds me of the movie *Schindler's List.* At the end of that movie, Schindler is standing there and he had bought all these Jews so that they could escape the camps. He had extravagant taste, but he had sold almost everything he owned. He was standing there and he was looking at all of them and he said, "See this ring? This could have been three more." He looked at his car and he said, "That could have been ten more lives! How can you put a price on a life? Why did I keep all of this?" That was so powerful.

Maybe that trophy really is a great thing because maybe that symbolizes the lives that have been changed by the dedication to Christ. Maybe that's what that means—not something for us, but something for God.

Morgan Cryar speaks to that man or woman who may have heard about Jesus, but never made a decision to follow Him.

Morgan Cryar

If you've never thrown yourself on the mercy of God, there's nothing you need more than to do that. I've concluded that I'm very much in need of God's forgiveness, and the Scripture says we all are. But God is very willing to do just that; in fact, He went to a lot of trouble just to pay for our sins. Turn toward God and ask for mercy. He is rich in mercy.

Michael O'Brien tells us that people write the songs, but God moves through them. With the help of the Holy Spirit and friends, here's what Michael learned.

Michael O'Brien

The year of 1996 was a time of discipline, a time of finding out who I was and why I was in Christian ministry. I found out that you can get caught up in the whole swing of Christian music: being an artist, having people know your songs and putting you up on a pedestal, and thinking it's all about you. I found out that I was building the Cause of Michael O'Brien instead of the Cause of Christ. It was a hard time for me. I felt like such a hypocrite. But when God showed me the greatness of my sin, then I was able to see the greatness of His love. He told me that no man was in control of what I did. So then my fear of rejection was released. He told me that the Holy Spirit was the one who moves a man to repentance, not me. He can choose when and where He is going to do that. I just have to be obedient. The songs on the record were inspired by God through sermons or personal testimonies, yet He can take it and use it for something I never thought possible. Just like the Word of God can speak to us even though it was written nearly two thousand years ago. He can even use someone whose heart is in the wrong place. I was a living testimony to that. My gifts are in music, but my calling is the same as every other Christian: to tell the world the Good News of Jesus. Hallelujah.

The altar call at the end of the night is an integral part of many Christian concerts. Amy Morriss reveals why she has always made it a part of her show.

Amy Morriss

There's a place in my concert, usually right before the last song, where I give the plan of salvation. There's an opportunity for people to come to know the Lord. If it's my concert I always do that. I ask them to slip their hands up so I can pray for them. I did that one night at a concert, and I didn't see any hands. I thought, *Well, I know the Lord was here, and He's working. There are things He did, I just don't know about it.* After the concert, a woman came up to me with her little boy. She was crying, and he was kind of looking shy. She said, "I want you to know, I have four children. My three oldest have been saved for a while, but tonight my little 7-year-old, our last one, got saved here at this concert. I want you to know how thrilled we are."

That is what it's all about. That is the very reason that I believe the Lord has called me to do this. When I was saved it was through a family that sang. It was through a person's ministry. [Now He's called me] to reach out to people who don't know Him and hopefully to encourage people who do.

Excited by the Word of God, the phenomenally successful group Point of Grace talks about the need to stay grounded in God's life-giving message.

Point of Grace
(Denise Jones, Shelley Breen, Heather Floyd, Terry Lang)

Shelley: We met with a lady in Houston named Beth Moore; she's been commissioned by the Southern Baptist Convention to write in-depth Bible studies for women. When she was finishing up the last Bible study that she was writing called "Jesus—The One and Only," she said the Lord just told her right then, "Give this to My girls." He was talking about us. "They need it."

It was the weirdest thing because it was perfect timing. We had been out on the road so much. It is always a wonderful experience to be able to be out and meet so many people, but after a while you feel kind of like a dry well. You're not in church every single Sunday, because you're singing at a different church every single Sunday. So we were feeling kind of empty. We go to Bible study when we're at home on Tuesday nights when we can, but sometimes we're not at home on Tuesday nights so we don't have any form of consistency or structure other than what we would make up for ourselves. So this was great. We've finished the first five weeks and now we're starting on the second five weeks. I remember her saying, "If you stay in the Word this much, being out on the road, this is going to save your neck." She was right. It's given us so much more strength. It comes from the preeminence of Christ, from eternity to eternity.

Denise: It's scary how in this Bible study you get to know Jesus Christ so personally, because she takes you from the preeminence, when it was just Him and God. Now we're almost to the crucifixion. [We've gone through] His childhood and all the miracles that He did. It's just incredible. You get to know Him so personally. It was perfect timing for us to get to know Jesus on a more personal level. One thing Beth said when we had that meeting was, "You remember when Moses went into the wilderness for forty days and forty nights and he saw God? When he came back he had no clue, but his face was glowing. I just want you girls to know that your faces are still glowing." *And we were all bawling!* That's what we needed to hear.

Shelley: We were feeling so tired and worthless at the time. Like, what are we doing out here? We're singing these songs, going through the motions, then all of a sudden, we woke up one morning and we felt like a dry well. It happened to us all at the same time. So it was good for somebody to say, "Don't let all the busyness feel like that's taking your motives away." Because the reason we started all this is because we love people. "Don't let Satan tell you you don't love them anymore. You still want to be out there doing what you do."

Soul2Soul: What's the message of Point of Grace?

Terry: What we always try to leave is encouragement. You know that you can make it through this stuff that you don't think you can, and you can make it through with a good attitude, and you can make it through with God. You can read your Bible and you can pray and it's going to be okay. It doesn't have to be awful. You can be content.

I think, too, that we really like to have fun. In concert we have this medley thing we do . . .

Heather: Where we make fools of ourselves!

Terry: Yeah, it's so good to see people laugh and smile and have a good time. They need to know that it doesn't have to be [sternly], "Okay, we come to church, we sing our hymn." We can have fun and we can laugh. I think sometimes some of those people haven't laughed in church in years. They see that there's joy in Christ. We can laugh and have a good time and celebrate through our troubles.

By staying in the water of the Word, Point of Grace is able to bring encouragement and a much needed sense of optimism to others. When the group Virtue searched for their message, they learned that growing up in a Christian home and being a light to others is a message.

Virtue

People ask us all the time who we're trying to reach. We like to say that there are three groups of people that we feel our ministry is for.

First of all, it's for those who are saved just to celebrate how good the Lord is. Every day that's what we do when we're singing our songs. All four of us have been raised in the Church all of our lives.

So second, and this is especially my burden, it is for people who have been raised in the Church, who go to church and participate out of habit, but haven't formed a relationship with God. When we first started we felt kind of intimidated because we couldn't go out on the stage and say, "You know, I've been out on the street, or the Lord delivered me from drugs," or that kind of thing. So we really struggled with, What do we have to say? What personally can we say? Overwhelmingly, we decided the thing that we've learned is just how wonderful the Lord is when you form a relationship with Him yourself.

This ministry, before it ever touched anyone else, before the album was ever released, touched the four of us, and we have grown spiritually so much just through what we've gone through so far developing that relationship. What we really want to send out to other people is: If you don't know Him for yourself, don't think that just because you sit in church every week, that that's really what it's all about. Because it's not about religion as much as it is about a relationship with Christ.

Third, and very important, it's the world: those people who aren't saved. As we do concerts and as we go to different cities, we want to encourage people to bring unchurched friends, unsaved people, to the concerts with them because we think that our music has the power to reach other people who haven't been introduced to the gospel before.

If you want to find out what is important to someone, look at where they invest their time and their resources. The Imperials have been making music for decades. Here they reveal what drives them as a group.

The Imperials

(Armond Morales, David Will, Jeff Walker, Steve Ferguson)

David: The whole thing is driven by ministry. All the rest of it can become mechanical. You can get tired just being on the road. Music's a wonderful thing, but it's a tool for us to spread the gospel, and it's the gospel that's the drive. That's the thing that motivates me to get out there. There's not enough of the other stuff to keep me motivated. It's seeing people's lives changed by the power of God and having God's music (because it is His music; He invented it) to use to minister to people. That is what really motivates me.

We're not always sure what it is that a person stands for anymore. If you find it refreshing when someone stands up for what they believe, get ready to be refreshed. There's no confusion about Angelo Petrucci's message.

Angelo & Veronica

(Angelo Petrucci, Veronica Petrucci)

Angelo: The world can preach about their buddha. They can preach about all their gods, but if we mention Jesus they suddenly say, *"We don't want to hear it!"* It's very frustrating to me because I'm a bold kind of character. I'm going to tell you about Jesus. I want you to know about my Jesus. Many of today's artists address issues that are happening in our country and in the world. I say, "Yeah, but there's no solution. You're addressing all these issues; but *there's no answer!* I have the answer. His name is Jesus."

Why can't we talk about God? Why are our voices muted when we talk about our God? When you talk about your god, you can boast about it, you can have videos on it, you can pollute young kids' minds with it. Our God stands for everything that is good, and that's the truth. You just open up the Word of God and read through it and you'll find out how good my God is. That's frustrating to me. My experience with God was powerful, especially because I was in the world for so long. So when I came to God, there was no turning back; there is no turning back in my life because I've seen what the world's got. The world's got nothing. Money? Cars? Boats? You know what? *They're all going away.* When you die, you'd better be storing up something a lot deeper than your bank account. You'd better be storing up stuff that's more significant than your fame. You'd better be focusing on it, because it's going to come to an end. And when it does, you'd better know where you're going.

"Overnight" successes rarely happen overnight. Behind the scenes and away from the spotlight, artists are growing. Anointed tells how the Lord has got to move in them in order for them to be able to be anointed.

Anointed

(Da'dra Crawford Greathouse, Steve Crawford, Denise "Nee-C" Walls)

Da'dra: It's interesting how we all view the success of different artists, ministries, and people as an "overnight" success. Often what we find out when we really talk to people is that they have really been in preparation for a long time. A lot of people think, *Oh, you guys have two records out*—when really we have three and we've been together for eight years.

I know we're all grateful for that process because the growth can happen so quickly. You don't want the ministry to grow faster than you grow. You need to grow along with the ministry so that you can *stand* on that level of the blessing. With every level of blessing comes a greater level of responsibility. I think as a group right now we're really humbled by what the Lord has done in our lives individually. He's got to move in us in order for us to be able to do the kind of music that we do so that people can feel the genuineness and the sincerity of what we write, sing, and say. We just want people to be blessed; we always have. It's always been our intention to be encouraging to people, to be uplifting and edifying to them, to be inspiring and to give hope to the hopeless and let them know that Jesus Christ is the way.

Nee-C: That's why we are here: *to pour* into these people's lives. Not necessarily to point a finger in their face, judging them and condemning them because they don't know the Lord and don't have Him in their life and they're not living the lifestyle we think they should be living.

We, as a people of faith, sometimes it just takes our lifestyle—living our life in front of them—to be a witness to them. Sometimes we're the only experience of Christ that they will ever see or ever have.

Da'dra: The analogy of a physical prison is very similar to being a prisoner in your soul and in your spirit, being bound inside to sin. The enemy will try to keep you from being all that God wants you to become in this world. We all believe that everyone born into this world has a purpose. The enemy's job is to keep you from fulfilling that purpose, but God is much greater than the enemy! The Word of God says, "*Greater is He that is in you, than he who is in the world,*" and "*You can do all things through Christ.*" We have been in places [performing] where we have been surrounded by nonbelievers. But where else can a light shine but in darkness? That is where the light is needed. Jesus even said, "The well don't need the physician, it's the sick that need the physician." Christians, we are not the people to take it upon ourselves to be self-righteous and we're so holy we just need to keep our holiness in our little corner. God said to go into all the world and to preach the gospel. That preaching the gospel can come in different forms. That's what I love about the body of Christ. Everybody has their own unique way, I believe, of getting the gospel across to someone. It takes the leading of the Holy Spirit and the wisdom of God. And God will lead you as to what someone else may need from you when you want to offer them Christ.

They call it the Good News, but why? Surely, our forgiveness and our salvation come to mind quickly, but Christ's comfort and our trusting Him are wonderful gifts that He also gives to us who believe. Janet Paschal helps us remember our God is a loving God who knows the future and cares about us immensely.

Janet Paschal

We never know what twelve months will hold. We never know the joys; we never know the challenges. I don't know if people who are important to me will be handed diagnoses that are not good. I don't know if there will be born another Mother Teresa or another Billy Graham or John Wesley. We don't know. We just don't know. But what we do know is that a long time ago He knew what the twelve months would hold. He knew the good and the bad and the challenges and the sorrows and the joys and *He won't be surprised by any of it.* Whether it's walking over a grassy knoll in a family cemetery or whether it's holding this brand-new creature that has your eyes or your jaw line. He won't be surprised by it.

That's what comforts me in looking at a new year. I mean it's always exciting, but you know sometimes the phone's going to ring and your world's going to turn upside down. That's inevitably going to happen. But the good thing is that it won't shock Him. It won't set Him back. He won't say, "Oh, I never expected that." He's already working on making it all work for our highest good. Not necessarily our ease or satisfaction, but He has His hands in the mix.

It's comforting. I think the older I get the more comforting it is to me. As you get older you realize that there are things that you cannot change. There are things that you cannot do within yourself. When you're young, everything seems possible. Then you get older and a lot of truths kind of settle in. For me, that's when it's been so comforting to say He is a lot smarter than I am, He knows me better than I know myself, and He cares *so much* about the ins and outs of my today and my tomorrow and my next week. I have to trust Him for that.

Christian comedian Chonda Pierce was a guest on *Soul2Soul* early in 1998. Besides making us laugh, she let us in on the secret of finding a message in the song of laughter.

Chonda Pierce

Timing as a comedian is everything. You find a story, you set it up, tell a punch line, and then hopefully people laugh. And life is like that: An event happens, you weed through the details, and finally God will send a punch line along so you can laugh. I heard the old saying, "Time heals all wounds." I've decided *time* doesn't heal anything. It's what God does during that time that we're waiting. That's when the healing comes and we can laugh again.

"For God so loved the world He gave His only begotten Son, that whosoever believes in Him should not perish, but have everlasting life." It's the message that we live and the message that we speak. But how will anyone hear it unless someone comes to tell it?

4 THE ROAD

"But tonight when it's quiet and I lie here alone,
I wish I was holding you so.
There's a price that I've paid for this life that I've made.
What price? Well, they call it 'The Road.'"

B. A. Beethoven, "The Road"

THERE'S A BIG PURPLE BUS with a Phoenix painted on it parked in front of a Shoney's somewhere in Nashville. It's Saturday morning about 9:00 A.M. and you are a Christian recording artist about to climb on board to start your commute to work. Okay, it's a little weird that your job is 340 miles away and you won't be back until Christmas, but other than that, it's a lot like what other people do.

Welcome to the road. If you're a Christian artist, this is where you live. Artists spend more time on a bus than Keanu Reeves in the movie *Speed.* It's the means of getting to where the people are that you will sing for, minister to, and talk with. It's the place where traveling artist and stationary public meet on common ground to get together, to share, to be inspired, to worship, and to celebrate.

Let's face it, you and I are not touring artists. We see concerts only from the vantage point of the auditorium. The cheap seats. We've never known the thrill of a great performance or the disappointment of a bad night.

Since every Christian artist travels, we have heard many stories from the road, and this chapter is full of such stories. Some are funny, others poignant, still others, personal—about the challenges to maintain the focus on what you're called to do, when it's difficult sometimes remembering even what city you're in.

I admire a lot of things about life on the road. There are times when groups support each other "out there." When one artist's well gets a little dry, another will pray and help fill it back up again. I wish we all had that. And I admire the camaraderie that must exist in a group of people all traveling together for weeks at a time.

The reality of course is that without actually being a Christian artist traveling on the road, we'll never know exactly what it's like. I hope this chapter will put you so close to the life on the road you'll think you hear amplifier hum. So grab a window seat on the bus. We've got forty-five cities to hit and just twelve weeks to do it in.

Tammy Trent

I've definitely been an artist, even before I had a record deal, who honestly would sing wherever God opened a door. Especially in Michigan before I was signed, I would sing at the weirdest places. I had never heard of a "hollar." Do you know what a hollar is? It was out in the middle of nowhere, and you had to walk out into the woods through the mud and over these creeks, around this bend and *up this tree and down that tree!* These bedsheets were hung up everywhere. I didn't know what a hollar was, so I'm like, "Great, I've got a good gig tonight. I'm going to sing at a hollar!"

So bedsheets are everywhere. I'm covered in mud. We come out, and they're cooking a pig over to the left. They've got turkeys on the right. They got a big ol' bonfire in the middle, and I get up and I'm *jamming* to "Someone to Love." They brought their boom box to sing with, and I was so grateful to be there. Mosquitoes were everywhere; I was eaten alive. The people, though, were precious. I think I sang until about one o'clock in the morning. We jammed to "Someone to Love," and "Your Love is 4 Always," and "Emotional," and it was really a blast. It could have been my worst gig, but I look at those moments and say, "You know what, these are awesome memories I'm creating at *the hollar!*"

Once upon a time long, long ago, the group 4 HIM was a brand-spanking new, untested musical act. Then they lugged their own equipment from town to town, singing their songs and sharing their faith. Now 4 HIM is at the top of the heap. Mark Harris says that "all the stages in their career have been enjoyable and frustrating at the same time." Today their days are filled with industry responsibilities, new record promotions, and hectic mega-meet-and-greets. I asked them if they missed anything from the good ol' days, and to share their worst concert experience and their most unforgettable.

4 HIM

(Marty Magehee, Kirk Sullivan, Andy Chrisman, Mark Harris)

Kirk: I don't miss the dog of a bus that we had and all of the driving that we did. All of our clothes, products, and luggage were on top of the bus with us on an all-night drive sleeping. Our sound equipment on the bottom was swinging in our faces. When it rained it would drip down on my forehead. We had eight bodies in a six-foot-long space, packed in like sardines. Man, we were right next to one another.

I would be less than human if I said that I didn't enjoy getting to ride in good buses now. We have a bus driver and people who set up the sound equipment. That lets us focus more on what we've been called to do instead of setting up the sound equipment, doing the concert, and then knowing halfway through the concert that, "Wow, for the next two hours after the concert we're going to tear this stuff down and load it into the trailer."

Mark: All of the different stages have been enjoyable and frustrating at the same time. The best concert was the first concert that we ever did because there were so many questions as to whether or not this would actually work. We played at First Baptist in Stockville, Mississippi. The youth pastor brought us in, and we had no idea how things would go that night. I remember at the end of the evening we gave an invitation. The building was fairly full, and that was a surprise, but the most surprising thing for us that night was the fact that we had so many wonderful decisions. Young people walked down and made commitments to Christ, and so I think for us that was one of the most important concerts. Maybe it wasn't the best concert we've ever had or the most enjoyable, but it was the most important because at that moment we realized that the anointing was on what we were doing and the Lord was using it to reach people. It was the first time we had seen that.

Marty: One of the most disappointing turnouts that we ever had was in Canada. This was the first chance for the guy in charge to promote anybody. We were at this church that sat about 3,600 people. Carman had been there a few weeks before and packed it out. People were standing everywhere and they crammed like 4,000 in there. The guy who was promoting promised us that there was no way that he could advertise. There was no radio station into the area. There was nothing. I remember we walked in the place and set up and the rest of the guys were flying in because this was our first concert back. After we got sound check going, it was getting late and it was time for us to eat. The guys were almost there so I asked, "Hey, where's dinner going to be?" And he said, "Oh, so you guys wanna eat?" So I knew that something was not too cool. Then that night in this big auditorium there were about 200 people who showed up and sat in the middle. In a 3,600-seater, 200 people is just a little, "yeaah!"

Afterward, we were talking to the people, and this woman came up and wanted me to sign a bumper sticker. I turned it over and was writing on it. She said, "I wish you guys would have let us know you were coming. I would have advertised it on the radio." I said, "The radio?" She said, "Yeah, turn the bumper sticker over." I turned it over and there was the logo of the university radio station, the big Christian radio station that had promoted Carman and everybody else. I thought, *Yeah, I wish I would have known.*

You know you're in trouble if you look out of the bus window fifteen minutes before the concert and wonder if there's another parking lot somewhere.

Another tour teamed up Greg Long, 4 HIM, and 1997 New Artist of the Year, Jaci Velasquez. If you think touring is all work and no fun, think again.

Jaci Velasquez

We had a phenomenal time. It was just so much fun! God really moved in so many neat ways. I had never seen 4 HIM in concert, and Greg and I were just amazed at the anointing God put on them. The last night, Greg and I were sitting down at the table in the bus, trying to figure out what we were going to do to them. We had to do something to them on the last night of the tour. We came up with this idea.

You know that song "There Is Shelter in the Rain"? Well, for that song we had five super-soakers stationed at each corner of the stage. After the second chorus, the super-soakers started squirting all four guys, literally just soaking them. These were huge super-soakers, so they carried tons of water. So through the whole song until the end, they were shooting them, shooting at the lights so that it would look like rain falling down. All you see are Andy and Marty rubbing their faces, rubbing the water from their eyes, trying to sing. It was so funny! My mother was blowing bubbles behind the stage so it would look like all this water and bubbles everywhere. We were throwing confetti at them at the same time. Toward the end of the song, Greg and I walked on stage behind them, twirling an umbrella and mimicking the dance steps they were doing. The crowd started laughing and all the guys looked back and saw us mimicking them with an umbrella so we wouldn't get wet. Oh, we had such a great time!

The open road. All of that freedom and yet, aboard the crowded tour bus there's nowhere to go. The Newsboys give us their view when the road gets too long and just physically tiring.

The Newsboys
(John James, Jeff Frankenstein, Peter Furler, Jody Davis, Duncan Phillips, Phil Joel)

Jeff: You look at our schedule, we're probably one of the most psychotouring bands in Christian music. In '95–'96 I think we did around 400 shows. Yeah, it does get very tiring sometimes, but in our case we really enjoy it. We feel so privileged that we have all become such good friends. That's just the way it has to be when you're on the road that much. If you're not like that it makes it extremely difficult. Of course, it's very hard being away from our families and our homes. You miss everybody while you're away and some days you wake up and you have no idea where you are or what time it is or how long you've been gone! You seriously don't know what day it is. Those things are tough, but the rewards are great.

And there are times when touring is emotionally draining. Artists often must rely on others to replenish their spirits.

Michael O'Brien

There are times when you are out on the road and you just don't have the strength. Sometimes you just don't feel like ministering. You could be going through personal problems at home or being attacked by Satan with negative thoughts like, "You are nothing. You aren't making a difference." It's a situation where you become weak. I am human, but I have the power to overcome these attacks. I have the authority to take these thoughts captive and make them obedient to Christ. That is when I have to be honest with whoever has brought me in. I tell them I am feeling down and I need prayer. I have to be honest about what I am going through. This is reality. It is going to happen, but how I deal with it can change the way I minister that evening. A lot of times I have found that God sends someone to serve my need, even when I haven't asked Him to. I am out there for no other reason than to bring the light of Jesus to a darkened world. And I pray that at the end of each concert, when they are given the opportunity to respond, the lost will be found in Christ Jesus.

Because traveling is sometimes very difficult, when the members of Anointed are asked how they can best be prayed for, they ask for strength and endurance.

Anointed

(Da'dra Crawford Greathouse, Steve Crawford, Denise "Nee-C" Walls)

Steve: Being on the road is very exhausting spiritually. It takes a lot of discipline because we don't really get a chance to be at our home church in Nashville often because we're usually en route somewhere from a place coming back and we'll get back too late for church or something. So I think our prayer would be for people to pray for us for strength, endurance, perseverance, and for unity and for love and for the Lord's will to continue to take preeminent place in our lives. That the vision that God has given us would continue to be fulfilled. It's amazing because His vision is continuing to be revealed and it's like, "more, more, more, more!" so that God would keep us in a place of humility. Because, only in humility can He exalt you in due time. And even that exaltation is for Him to be exalted! When He exalts you it just gives you a platform to give Him the glory.

There are lessons from the road that apply to us even if we are not recording artists. Bruce Carroll tells stories about trusting God when it seemed to make no sense at all and keeping our sense of humor.

Bruce Carroll

It's interesting that some of the best gigs were not the ones with the most people or the best sound or whatever. It was the time that God seemed to show up in a very special way.

There was a night when I was healed in Columbus, Ohio. I left Nashville by faith and flew to Ohio to do a concert. I left by faith because I was really sick. I was just feeling terrible. I was hoarse, couldn't talk. I thought, *This is nuts! I should call the guy and cancel this gig.* But I just didn't have any peace about it at all. Neither did my wife and I always check with her to make sure I'm hearing God or not hearing Him. I said, "Nikki, I don't really feel I'm supposed to cancel this date. But I feel terrible and can't talk, much less sing. What do you think?" And she said, "I know you're supposed to go."

Anyway, I went. The Lord miraculously healed me when I got out on stage. That was an awesome night. It was amazing to be healed because it had never happened to me like that. That was a real life-changing kind of thing. The funny thing was that after the concert I couldn't talk. It was almost as if God were saying, *"You know, I can do anything I want to do, whenever I want to do it. This is a lesson in stepping out in faith and believing that it's all about Me and not about you, and I can do whatever I want to do."* Which is why we should all always be willing to step out in faith because this may be the time that God wants to do something. Peter never got the opportunity to walk on water until he got out of the boat.

On the other hand, one of the worst concerts was somewhere down in Mississippi. You know, it was just train wreck after train wreck. I forgot the words, the lights broke, the sound geeked, and . . .

I broke a string. I was on this small stage that was in a gymnasium. I had broken a B string and so I got a B string out of my case in front of everybody and was unwrapping it when it popped out of the wrapper and flew behind the stage down a four-inch space—and I was about four feet off the ground. It popped right into that little space. So I had to crawl on my belly and reach down behind the stage to get that string in front of everybody!

And it was a real nondemonstrative crowd. Nobody was moving. It was like an oil painting, and I was dying up there. I changed the string, stalled for time, and finished my gig, but it was pretty harrowing.

Every artist and Christian group has their own idea of the ministry God has called them to. I appreciate the enthusiasm of the father and son group Aaron-Jeoffrey. They place a premium on ministry and trust that God is pleased when they enjoy it.

Aaron-Jeoffrey

Jeoffrey: This is what we do; we're called to the ministry. Artistry? Yeah, it's very important that we keep on the cutting edge of our artistry, but really the thing we're about is ministry.

Aaron: And people.

Jeoffrey: We write the best songs we can write, find the best songs we can find, and use the best producers that we can possibly afford. We want to get to be the best that we can be, not to compete with anybody else, but just to be the best that we can possibly be.

The first place Jesus took the disciples was to a party! So our concerts are like a party; it's up, it's fun, it's a journey to the person of Jesus. So you say, "*Oh, you mean God really digs it when we have fun? God really enjoys us enjoying ourselves?*" Yeah, I think He really does. And you say, "*God really likes our music?*" Yeah, He really does.

We might imagine what it would be like to travel the world sharing the life-changing message that Jesus Christ loves us and wants to give us hope and a future. Like many Pam Thum stories, there's a wealth of richness beneath the surface. In this story, Pam went to South Africa to help raise up the next generation, only to find some of them are already there.

Pam Thum

I just got back from South Africa. In fact, I was in South Africa and then instead of coming home they took me directly on the road to sing for ten more days. I just got home two days ago. That was a wonderful trip! It was so exciting that I can't even tell you. I premiered a new song called "There's a Future for the World."

It was at a world conference where 35,000 people were involved from 132 countries. I had two great big adult choirs and a children's choir singing with me. It's a song I wrote for South Africa. At the beginning there's a Zulu choir chanting, in Zulu, Jeremiah 29:11, which says, "God has a future, a hope in good things . . ." It was really one of those wonderful moments when you think, *I just want to save this moment* because it was 132 countries coming together at this convention asking, "How can we tell the world that God is a good God by the year 2000? That He's a God who loves us and wants to give us hope and a future?"

As I stood there and looked out at the crowd, and I looked around to the children's choir, their faces were so filled with hope and faith. And as I talked to the children, there was one little boy, 7 years old. I had a sore throat. I don't know what possessed me, but I asked, "Honey, would you pray for me and my throat?" And he just took off praying, "In the name of Jesus, I just rebuke you, Satan! Cover her with the love of Jesus!" I was opening my eyes, thinking, *Oh my goodness, this is our future*. The world says that young people are not standing up for the Lord. And I'm saying, "Oh no, they are." Here's this 7-year-old boy saying, "I'm confident that God has a future for me. I'm confident that Jesus knows where I am." It was just a really thrilling moment.

There's a single question in interviewing applied to all topics of questioning: Why? In this case, what makes you go out and perform a hundred nights a year? Wayne Watson understands exactly why he still does this after all these years.

Wayne Watson

If I were just going out a hundred nights a year to play to entertain people, I think I would miss my family too much to do that. I don't begrudge anybody who wants to do it, but for me I enjoy being home too much to go away just to make people laugh, tap their feet, or clap their hands for a few hours. I enjoy the fact that there is some potential for eternal change every night in our concerts. Whatever we do, whether it's a church service, a Bible study, or a prayer service, there is always in those situations the potential for eternity, for someone in that setting to be changed. That excites me, and that's pretty much what motivates me to still do it after all these years.

There's a pie that drives me. It has three pieces. One piece is the entertainment slice—I don't deny that what we do is somewhat of an entertainment-based industry, if you want to call it that. But you know, my pastor is entertaining. Most pastors I hear are entertaining to some degree. I don't think that's a negative thing as long as it's not the biggest piece of the pie. It's a small slice.

There's a vocational slice in that this is what I do to provide a living for my family, and God has blessed us more than I ever dreamed possible. I never had ambitions to do this so it's not like I've been chasing some dream and finally we are about to catch it or have caught it or whatever.

As long as the biggest slice of that pie remains ministry and eternal in nature—that drives me. No matter how many times I sing a particular song. I may think, *I'm so tired of this song.* I've been playing one for fifteen years. I've been playing another for ten years. I really get tired of singing this and some nights I think, *Let's don't do that one. I don't feel like doing that one tonight.* But there are people in the audience who may need that one. I try to be spiritually sensitive and listen to the Lord speak to me and say, "Go ahead and do it!" Even in the middle of a concert, I'll go ahead and put things in or take things out because I think that's what Spirit-led living is about. Not just at the beginning of the day, but through the day and through the night—to listen to His voice. That drives me. I realize what we're singing has potential to impact somebody's life and decisions they make about their lives.

Whiteheart stands as one of the foremost Christian rock groups of all time. During their fifteen years as a group they have earned forty top ten singles and twenty-one number one songs. After performing thousands of notable concerts all over the world, Whiteheart shared one for the record books.

Whiteheart

(Billy Smiley, Mark Gersmehl, Rick Florian)

Mark: We were playing in Norway. I love Norway. Norway is one of the greatest countries on the earth. It's just a sensational place and I love the people. We'd played there before at a camp and done some seminars and I was looking so forward to going there.

When we got to the airport in Nashville, our drummer seemed to be unaware that a passport was a necessity for traveling overseas. He seemed to have somehow misplaced his. When we arrived he said, "I don't have my passport." (And you're going to be doing *what* for the next few days?) So he goes. We fly into Chicago and he tries to go downtown to the passport office, and of course it doesn't work. We leave and fly off to London, waving good-bye to our drummer at the concourse. He is now staying in Chicago and we're going to Norway—those cities *really* aren't all that close.

We fly through London, arrive in Norway, and we're thinking, "What are we going to do?"

Rick: In a Rock and Roll band you can really use drums!

Mark: Then the airline hasn't found it in their hearts to bless us with our own clothing or equipment. So we stayed there in the airport for three more hours trying to find our clothes. We're supposed to play at nine o'clock that night—there's nothing there. We have to drive three hours to get to the venue. Finally, we leave without our gear, without our clothes, and without a drummer. We get to the venue and, fortunately, our road manager also played drums.

Billy: We think.

Mark: He hadn't played in over two-and-a-half years . . . but he *said* he played drums so we said "OK, you're in."

We get out on stage, and I was wearing what I wore on the plane. Rick had gotten a shirt from somebody else.

Rick: The audience would throw things up on the stage so that I would have something to wear. (They had learned what had happened.)

Mark: The people were great! But we start the song, and I looked over at Rob, our road manager, sitting behind the drums, and we're all thinking, "Okay, we got about 10 bars in and we're still all in the same measure together. We're going to be alright here." You know what? For not having played in two-and-a-half years, he did an unbelievable job. But the funny thing is . . . drumming is a very physical thing to do. And by the end of the night we're playing "Independence Day" which is off the *Powerhouse* record, and we're at the end. It was just unbelievable because the verses were *kicking away*, and when we get to the chorus I looked over at him. You know it was like watching the Boston marathon and you're seeing that guy who's about to collapse over the tape. This is him. Literally, by the time we get to the first chorus, we have dropped 15 beats per minute. You can just see the tempo sliding downhill. I look over at him and I can visibly see his forearms swelling; he is Popeye by the end of the song. He was half dead sitting on the drummer's stool. We absolutely loved him for doing that, but I don't think we'll be playing in Norway anytime soon.

Newsong performs about 170 concerts per year. That's roughly one concert every other day, plus travel. In our interview the topic of motivation arose. Evidently, it's a popular question, but we had to ask it too.

Newsong
(Eddie Carswell, Billy Goodwin, Leonard Ahlstrom, Scotty Wilbanks, Russ Lee)

Scotty: The biggest question we get asked is, What is your motivation? How do you leave your families and your kids to get on a bus and travel across the country? Each one of us obviously has been called into the ministry or else we wouldn't be here.

I had a guy tell me one time, "Man, if you think you've been called into the ministry, really pray about it because if you get out there you're going to be miserable if you haven't been called to it." We know that God's placed a calling on each one of our lives to spread His Word with the talents and the abilities that He's given us.

That's what motivates us. That's what fuels our engine. That and then night after night seeing God just show up and work in people's lives, changing hearts and turning people around. I think that's what motivates us to keep going to that next town and then to the next town.

Scotty Wilbanks says you've got to be cut out to be in a traveling music ministry. If you are called, it all comes together.

Greg Long

What's interesting now is that the recording aspect of what I do is, for me, just time standing still. Because of my background, the music ministry will always mean being on the road and traveling. Everything I do to prepare for the album, the recording, or the necessary promotions that go into it, is just the means to an end: to go back out on the road.

Eric Champion has transformed himself from teenage vocalist to alternative music pioneer. That change is evident in his music and in his growth as a performer as well.

Eric Champion

I love live concerts. I've done so many different types of things. There's been even a larger transformation in my live performance than in my recorded music. I remember starting out when there was just me and a Dat track. You can't do that anymore. Those were the good old days. I'll probably look back one day and say, "*I remember when I could get on a plane and take my little cassettes 'bout that size, take 'em to a church, pop 'em in and sing.*" That was quite easy. That didn't seem like work.

Man, I've had a lot of different experiences performing. I remember one thing that was incredible. My first album had come out and I was getting ready to do my first festival. It was out in San Bernadino, California. I was very starstruck being backstage in the catering tent and seeing all these people that I'd listened to and had their records growing up and discovering Christian music. Anyway, I got a chance to perform a song that night and it was my hit single. I remember seeing all these people who were singing the words, and it just shocked me. The last chorus was when I noticed it because I was so scared I was performing with my eyes closed. I didn't open my eyes until the last chorus to see what they were doing—to see if they were getting ready to throw tomatoes or something. I saw all these people singing, and it was just shocking to see people that knew your music.

I think right then I realized there's a big struggle even in Christian music: you have to daily remind yourself why you're doing this. It's such an easy thing, especially for a young performer, to think "*Wow, they're singing my songs. I'm pretty cool.*" Humility is a something you have to constantly deal with.

I'm having more and more fun performing now. For so long I kind of hid behind something, whether it be a keyboard or for awhile I was standing up and playing drums, then I had to learn to play the guitar just to be doing something other than just singing. Now that I'm traveling with this killer band I'm just singing and being able to perform. I've always loved theater, so I'm able to just have fun and try to get my songs across without having to be hampered by any instruments or anything. That's really fun.

Christian artists aren't just singing for the Church anymore. More often, they find themselves in places singing for people who might not otherwise hear them.

Angie & Debbie Winans

Debbie: We were invited to sing not long ago at a new restaurant that's up-and-coming. It's kind of in line with a Hard Rock Cafe and House of Blues. It's called BET Soundstage, and it's beautiful. It's high class, and it was a pleasure to be able to sing there.

The stage is right in front of an artsy bar, and Angie and I were trying to figure out which three songs from our album to sing. We said, "Should we do 'Never'?" *No, 'Never' is too hard.* We don't want to be hard." Angie's saying, "Not 'Natural'?" I said, "*No, let's not hit them that hard.*" You know, because the album had just come out, and that was like a promotional date. You know, you do want somebody to buy your album. So we'd say, "'Rebuke the Devil'?" "*No, it can't be 'Rebuke the Devil.*'" So Angie said, "Look. The whole album is forward, okay? We shouldn't have done it if we were going to be scared to sing it." So that's we said, "We didn't do it; God gave it to us. It's time to do what He told us to do and stand before the people." You can do nothing less than to give them what God said. They can't be mad at you because when God says do it, believe me He has set the grounds.

So we said, "All right, let's just pick three: 'Rebuke the Devil,' 'Love Won't,' and 'I Believe.'" We started "Rebuke the Devil," and I do the talking part at the beginning. I said, "Listen, I have something very important to say . . ." So I'm up there and I'm thinking, *Oh, my gosh, I'm about to [denounce] alcohol.* Angie could see it on my face. So she whispered in my ear, "Do what God says, girl, do what God says!"

Angie: I said, "His Word won't return void."

Debbie: Yeah, "His Word will not return void. Just do what God says." So I said, "Alcohol . . . it kind of takes away your better judgment." I was trying to be nice about it. Never-the-less, it was well received. People had to figure out what I was saying, but at the end just before we left we got a praise report that people stopped ordering drinks.

Angie: They were losing money.

Debbie: They started ordering Cokes, water, and orange juice. Management was saying, "I'm losing money here. Don't bring those girls on a Saturday night anymore." So when we left, we just rejoiced! We gave God much praise. Going out to the car, I said "Thank You, Jesus!" because His Word worked immediately. That's what they needed. They needed to know they had a choice. You do not have to take what the devil hands you. You can rebuke him and send him right back where he came from. You do not have to take what he gives you. That means somebody didn't drive home drunk. Somebody didn't have an accident, and we just have to give God the praise.

The growth curve Christian music is experiencing right now is exciting and amazes all of us working in and around it. Fortunately there are also many performers who remember the good ol' days of how this industry was born and how it grew up. Because the Spirit is always the same and doesn't suffer a season out of style, it's good to look back at the early days of Christian Rock (as it was called then) and consider the way from which we came.

Glad

(Chris Davis, Jim Bullard, Ed Nalle, John Gates, Paul Langford)

Ed: One of the great things about early contemporary Christian music, particularly in southern California, was that it was based out of the Church. Very often there was a speaker along with the group that went on the road with them. It was a ministry and the music became popular, but it was a result of a ministry as opposed to ministry being tacked on to music. That's one of the things that distresses me somewhat about what's going on in contemporary Christian music today. It's gotten so big and very commercial. There's nothing wrong with being commercial, with people liking what you do enough to buy it. That's wonderful, and we're glad that they do. But it gets back to your basic motivation for what you do. I hope that we can continue to be tied to the Church, because that's how it will work best. A big concert that blows through if it's not tied to the Church, people come to see it, but it hasn't got much lasting value. Whereas, if it's tied to the local church and someone does accept the Lord at one of our concerts, there's potential there for follow-up and growth. God can do all kinds of things in a person's life.

Here's another story about touring. It's one that doesn't make the papers, and generally, no one will get an award for it (not on earth anyway). I'd like to tell Brett that if he's trying to get rich and famous, he's going about it in the wrong way. Then again, I think he knows.

Brett Williams

We were in St. Petersburg, Russia, a while ago. We'd basically go out every morning, set up a sound system and the band, and play at the subway stop for five or six hours, draw people around, and then we'd share the gospel. Then we'd take down the gear, go eat dinner, set it up again, and do a concert that night. It was a way to draw people in, get them into a place where someone could go up and hand them a tract or share the love of Jesus Christ with them.

To me, that's the place to be. The local church is what God's using. I don't think He's necessarily using the Christian music industry. He's using Christians in the Church. To me, that's the safest place to be. I'm working with people in the Christian music industry who love the Lord, and they're plugged into the Church as well. But the industry itself, it's just a thing. It's not the Lord's Bride. So I just try to stay plugged into the local church. Anything I can do outside of that—the festivals, the recordings, and the videos, all that kind of stuff—I enjoy it tremendously.

It's a huge blessing and a big present from the Lord, but the real work's being done in the fellowships.

Music is a key opening the hearts of those who may have yet not heard the gospel. In this story the California group Rich Young Ruler accompanies three pastors to Japan to join hands with Japanese Christians there and tell their countrymen about Jesus.

Rich Young Ruler

(Rob Bender, Jennifer Bender, Erik Tokle, Mead Cheseboro, Ron Mukai, Garrett Burrow)

Mead: The crusades are set up for evangelism. With the language barrier, it's really hard to tell what's going on as far as a response. Japan is a very friendly country so we were never sure if the response to our music was out of them being nice or really genuine.

It was really cool. Half of one percent of Japan is Christian, so when you get an opportunity like that, it's awesome. I think the response was good. The venues were either small stadiums or concert halls. The events were promoted as concerts, not necessarily Christian oriented, but concerts, and that's how we would draw people out.

Rob: The name of the tour was "Gospelfest," and the headlining act, if you will, was a Black Gospel artist. For the audiences, he was the draw. We also had a Japanese singer with us who was also a pastor. So all together, there was Rich Young Ruler, the Gospel act, and someone singing Christian songs in the Japanese language. We traveled there with three pastors, so each night we would do our thing, another act would do their thing, the Japanese singer would sing, and then one of the pastors would speak and the message would be translated into Japanese. Then the translator who was also a Christian would speak and give an invitation.

Mead: It was really amazing every night we played because there was a huge response every night. You could see how the people came in and how they left changed by God. People got saved.

Rob: What was an equal blessing was to see the small contingency of people in the Church elated that all these Christians from America took the time to go there, stand beside them, and encourage them. And just to see a lot of their countrymen get saved.

For more than ten years, First Call has earned a reputation, first as a trio and later as a duo, for brilliant vocal arrangements and soul-penetrating songwriting. In terms of where they perform, they nourish connection by going wherever the people who love their music are.

First Call

(Marty McCall, Bonnie Keen)

Marty: We all tend to pay so much attention to what's going on in our country—the sales and the radio and all those things that are really exciting. We really love and appreciate them. But when you realize that there are things going on and there are people being ministered to *deeply* by these songs in other places that we've never been to or we haven't been very close to, it's overwhelming. We want to get there and be with those people.

We were singing songs at this huge concert in Puerto Rico, and they were all singing along! We had no idea that anyone was being ministered to by some of these older songs of ours. And the same thing with Canada. It's like here they are, our neighbors, and we kind of always think, *Oh, the Canadian market up there. That's Canada and they don't sell as many records as the States do.* But you go there and spend a little time with them and you realize that these are very real people who appreciate this ministry, and are affected by the songs, and have us in their homes through our recordings, and you want to get there and be with them. I think that's something new in our ministry too: our desire to be with the people who love our music. It's what the ministry aspect of what we're doing is all about, and it's really energizing us in a new way.

A concert tour isn't a finite event, lasting several months and then shutting down for the rest of the year. It is constant, and artists travel throughout the year, year after year. Artists who understandably want to see their families often take them along on the road. They stay together, supporting one another as they realize the work they are called to do.

Kim Boyce

We started back out on the road when my son was 3 months old. He's traveled with us ever since. I'm very blessed in that my husband travels with me. He sings backup vocals and has a new responsibility of driving the bus.

We bought a bus because at about 15 months it was no longer fun for my son to fly with us! Once he was mobile, keeping him corralled in an airplane seat just was not quite as much fun as it had been when he was really small.

We got a bus so that we could still travel as a family and take the band with us. Also to have a place that would feel like home for my son. We as a group and as a band have seen more children's movies than we ever dreamt possible, but it's been great. I've loved it, and it's been a wonderful time in my life.

In a certain way, I consider myself a working mom. I do have a career/ministry, but I'm very blessed. To a certain extent, I get to work out of my home, and when we're home, *we're home.* I may have to come do an interview, or run to the record company, or go sing a song or demo if I'm working on a new tune or something like that. But for the most part, when I'm home, I'm home. I'm blessed that when we pack up and go, we all go. Home sort of travels with us. Especially when we get on the bus, and it's the same bus: That's our bed and this is little Gary's place. That's where his toys are in that drawer. So, it's just been really the ideal situation for me to be able to continue to have my ministry, but at the same time to be able to spend the vast amount of time that I want to spend with my husband and my son. Gary and I sit down and we look at little Gary and we think, *This is all just going to be over way too fast.* It's flying by too quickly and we want to be there for as many of the seconds as we possibly can.

Out of the Grey takes great care in the recording studio, crafting their impeccable sound. But it's those times on stage with just the two of them—Christine singing and Scott on guitar—that give fans their biggest chills.

Out of the Grey
(Scott Dente, Christine Dente)

Christine: We definitely feel it when we're on stage and it's just Scott and me. We can play with dynamics like you just can't believe because we respond off each other. When you're with other players in the band, they're not as in tune to the ebb and flow of the song. So that's what we enjoy. When we play a song like "The Deep," we always play that acoustically. We can change it up night after night. He may make this section of the song quiet and I'll respond and get quieter and vice versa. It's really fun to do that.

Out of the Grey, like Kim Boyce, is a traveling family. I asked them what the first few minutes home coming off the road are like.

Christine: We walk in the door, and I start the washing machine.

Scott: I unload the cars.

Christine: The kids run around, and we get them juice. And for the next few days we thank the Lord that we have a home, that we have many modern amenities and enough money to buy good food. And then we gear up to get back on the bus.

Scott: One of the hardest things for Christine and me is to look at each other when we're out traveling. Not that we don't physically look at each other, but to really see each other. We're in survival mode a lot when we're on the road. We're seeing to the kids' needs, we're trying to do a good show, we're trying to keep our focus on why we're out there, and doing our job and performing well and taking care of all the million business things that need to be taken care of. So when we get home, a lot of times we'll look at each other and we'll say, "Oh, hi. Yeah, I remember you. We married each other and it's because we love each other." So there's a lot of re-hooking up for us when we get back. That's why we don't like touring for very long periods.

The road means many things. It's a highway of contradictions: fun and endless commuting, freedom and confinement, ministry and livelihood, doing what you love and wishing sometimes you were somewhere else entirely. Still at the end of the night, there's nothing left to do but play the song they all came to hear. For Phillips, Craig, & Dean, that's a song called "Concert of the Age."

Phillips, Craig, & Dean

(Randy Phillips, Shawn Craig, Dan Dean)

Dan: That one I've never tired of singing! There are some that I tire of singing, but not that one. For the last year or so it's been our closer.

Randy: It's up. People know the song and so they're usually singing along with us.

Shawn: Even sometimes quiet audiences will get into that song. The other night we had an audience that was fairly quiet. They were really into the music, but in different parts of the country audiences react in different ways. They had been kinda quiet until we got to the part in the song where it says, "*Across the sea of faces shout the praise* . . ." and they just started screaming! "WOOOO!!!!"

Randy: It scared me to death.

Shawn: I thought, *Man, they woke up.*

Randy: On our last song!

Shawn: It's been neat because when we first heard that song, Jackie Patillo [the former A&R executive at Star Song] kind of had to sell us on that. She was really fired up about that song; but I'm glad we did it.

Dan: Yeah, it's so visual and describes what a great scene it's going to be around the throne—not a real stale and formal concert.

Shawn: *It's going to be a celebration.*

Randy: It's going to be a great party. And we're going to be up there with three mics. [much laughter]

As you read this passage, countless touring buses are transporting Christian artists all across the country. But without songs to sing, there would be no concerts.

THUNDERBOLTS AND LIGHTNING:

THE WRITING OF MUSIC FOR GOD

> "Someday we'll be called to give an account, and I don't think our crown will be the music we wrote. I don't think our crown will be the words we wrote. I think it will be how we have built up the body of Christ, how we have torn down walls of suspicion and walls of fear, how we have shed light on false doctrines, how we've been encouraging truth, how that affects lives, and how we made Jesus visible."
>
> Rich Mullins

THEY SAY IN NASHVILLE, it all starts with a song. Before the recording sessions are booked or the concert tickets are put on sale, there's a songwriter writing a song.

The writing process is steeped in mystery. Just how do our favorite songs find their way from vague sketch to finished classic? How do artists translate their thoughts and emotions into lyrics and melodies able to move us so deeply?

Inside these songs lie the beliefs of Christians who best express their understanding of Christ through the fluidity of music. In them, we recognize the desire of the writers to voice their deep and personal faith in Jesus Christ. Rich Mullins said songwriters write "not because the world has need of your music; you write because you have a need to make order, to organize things."

Perhaps then singing the song is telling what's been organized, sharing what's coming together spiritually in their lives.

I'm not surprised that the artists, without completely understanding how the creative process works, have a rich body of opinion on the subject. One artist may say his experience is more hard work than flash of inspiration. Another artist told me, "All songs are written in heaven. God just gives them to us." It's fair to say that most songwriters are passionate about what they do. Every artist has his or her own approach to writing, and each song has its own story of how it was created. There's so much that could be said that this chapter could be a book in itself. The writing talent that resides within the Christian music community is underappreciated, even sometimes by those of us closest to it.

Stephen Curtis Chapman

My pastor, Scotty Smith, was on the Young Messiah tour. I was in the middle of this process of the recovery of passion within my own heart: wanting to write songs that would really reflect whatever it was God wanted me to say and feeling like I was running up against brick walls everywhere I turned.

And so I spent a lot of time on that tour with Scotty. We were just talking, throwing ideas around, and he was encouraging me. I would ask him questions, and we would dive into the Bible for a while and just had a great time. At one point I told him about a song I was working on. I had actually seen a title in a Max Lucado book: "Music for the Dance." I said, "I'm thinking about this song, and I've got a verse and I've got a chorus, but I come to that last part and all I can come up with is 'music for the dance,' but I'm not sure that's the thing." So we talked a little about it and he said, "*Well, it sounds like you're talking about the Lord of the Dance.*" It was that moment that bells and whistles went off, lightning flashed, and I said, "That's it!" What was so exciting was that song was a real turning point for the whole project [*Signs of Life*]. It was at that point where I went, "Wow, now I've got that new breath of fresh air to begin to create this album." So that song is really special because of that.

Rich Mullins always had an answer for every question he was asked. On the topic of songwriting, he qualified as an expert. The song "Awesome God" is undeniably a classic.

Rich Mullins

I think that listening is the better part of music. People will ask me how to become a good writer, and my general answer, not that I would know, but if I can be presumptuous enough to answer, is to be a good reader. The best way to become a good singer is to become a good listener. One of the wonderful things about teaching music is, I think, the things that are important in music are just important in life.

Expecting an *awesome* story, I asked Rich to tell how he wrote his most famous song, "Awesome God."

I was trying to stay awake. I was driving a little four-cylinder Ford Ranger and I had more weight than I could pull uphill. There's something really musical and kind of mystifying about the way that the more hallelujah kind of oriented preachers go at it. It's very rhythmic. It's very cool. So I was just kind of yelling Bible verses at cars as they would go by me, and that's how I wrote that.

It's a very boring story, and see, that's what nobody gets. Everybody thinks that writers sit around in this perpetual fog of inspiration, and it's really just a fog of confusion. Sometimes it's a caffeine buzz, you never know exactly what it is. I think that most people that write, if they were honest, wouldn't say, "Yes, God appeared to me and gave me this song." For me, my understanding of the way things work is that after God made man, He told him to reproduce and be fruitful. It's a wonderful command that I'm not allowed to follow because I'm not married. He also told us to subdue the universe. I don't think He meant to exploit it, but that we were to try to create order out of chaos and organize things. The first job He gave Adam was the job of naming the animals. The word there for "naming" really means to sort of categorize. He kind of says, "Call out what they are. Tell Me what these are." I think work is a very, very holy thing, and I take work very seriously. Most of us think that spiritual exercises are something you do once you get home from work, but I think what you do at your work is just as spiritual as the twenty minutes you have set aside to read Oswald Chambers. So for me, my songs are not a matter of something God has given me. I am grateful to God that He gave me ears, that He gave me parents who allowed me to take piano lessons, that He gave me some natural talent in the area of music. I'm very thankful to God that He gave me an environment to grow in where I was taught to listen and appreciate things. Then what I give Him back when I write a song like "*When he rolls up his sleeves he ain't just puttin' on the ritz*," that is my worship to Him, and I think He accepts it not because it's *great* music.

If you want to talk about *great music*, there was enough great music written by the time Bach died that none of us ever needed to pick up a pen and write a note. You don't write because the world has need of your music;

you write because you have a need to make order, to organize things. If you're a musician you express that very human, very common need by making music. If you're a baker, you do it by making bread. It's all the same goodness, it just expresses itself in different areas.

It's interesting to ask artists whom they are writing their songs for: Are they written for us exclusively, or are we peering inside an artist's private diary?

Bryan Duncan

I think I write all the songs to me at some point. It's God speaking to me, it's me speaking to God: "I've got to get You into my heart, out of my head." Most of the songs are dialogue between me and God, whether I tell you it's about Him or about me. In some ways, I'm talking to anyone who's listening: "Hey, tell me you don't sleep at night, I know"—I've been there. "Because of how things have been"—it's just easy to worry. So I'm talking to somebody else I guess. "Hey, things are going to change," that's what somebody told me. "It won't always be like this"—that's a piece of advice I was given. It got me through some really hard things where there was just nothing I could do. There are a lot of times you're just in a circumstance, and it's not going to go by any faster by hollering at it. And you can't fix it. It's like a rainy day—here it is. I just think that that song is just me talking to anybody else.

I haven't done a lot of songs from God's point of view because I really don't want to speak for God. *But you should hear the way God speaks to me.* It's not very flowery. The thing that just caught me when that came out in the bridge of the song ["Take Another Look at Me"] was, "I'm not surprised by the things you do and say." It really caught me off guard even when I wrote the lyrics down. "I'm not surprised." He's just saying, "You think I'm horrified that you had an evil thought? Do you think it really throws Me off that you're angry at Me? That you feel I didn't do the job right?"

I learned that God is not fragile. He can handle your discourse with Him no matter how heated you might get. If you've never been angry with God, you probably haven't spent any time with Him *'cause He's really opinionated!* That's kind of what I wanted to say in the song—[God saying] "Take another look at Me because you don't have a very good picture." And He's right—I don't have a good picture. It's like I was learning today, it's easy to see God as your parent and put Him in the place of your parents. At some point you can attach whatever personality that your parents had on God. There's a tendency to make some huge mistakes about the personality of God, if you base it too much on your parents. No matter how good your parents were, they're not God.

Bryan sheds a lot of light on the topic of where his songs come from. His communication with God became the basis for the song "Take Another Look at Me." Songs are sometimes simply personal revelations spoken to an audience through melody and musical arrangement.

Since the music of 4 HIM is so solid, it's interesting to find out what they see in their legacy of hit-making. What do they themselves hear in the work that they've created?

4 HIM

(Marty Magehee, Kirk Sullivan, Andy Chrisman, Mark Harris)

Andy: I think if you listen to our music, through the progression of albums, I think it's pretty clear that our music defines our Christian walk. I think you can see a heritage of what we're been through after seven years together. Basically, all we're singing about are things we've gone through. Mark writes the bulk of the songs, Marty writes some of the songs, and the reason we like to record songs that were written in the group is because that's where the heart comes out. We've been together so much. We've been together almost ten years. We've been through a lot together. When Mark writes a song or Marty writes a song, there's a pretty good chance it's going to be dealing with things we've all been through together.

I'm not quite sure we really knew what we were doing on the first record. We really trusted the Lord to bring the right songs to us. Every record after that I think you can see how our spiritual lives are growing and how we're dealing with our environment. You begin to see songs about children, provision for families, the intensity of the calling, and all those different things.

I think if there's one single thread that runs through our albums, especially from the second album on, you can see our Christian walk. I think you can see where it's grown, where it's changed, what our priorities are. And I think it's very evident in the straightforward lyrics that we sing.

If the lyrics tell the story of where the heart of the artist is, the melody lays its path into the soul of the songwriter. Michael W. Smith takes us to where the gift is celebrated and the music is born.

Michael W. Smith

To me it's a real gift to be able to sit down and close my eyes, place my hands on the keyboard and not know what they're going to go do. They just start doing something that

I've never done in my whole life. Suddenly I'm making music right on the spot. Sometimes I think, *Gosh, I love this. Lord, thank you. You gave me this gift. I pray that I can continue to glorify you with it.*

You start messing around and all of a sudden you come across this eight-bar phase that makes you go, "*Wow.*" One of those was "Place in this World", one of those was "Friends", one of those was . . . I mean, the list goes on. In all of my favorite songs, the music was written in less than five minutes. It just poured out of my fingertips and there it was. I feel almost guilty for taking credit for it. It's a phenomenon to me and very hard to put into words. I really don't understand how it happens. All I know is it's supernatural and it's the Lord.

Most artists have one song that stands out as their signature song. For Morgan Cryar, "What Sin?" is just such a song. Here he talks about it long before the rest of us had a chance to hear it.

Morgan Cryar

I really do believe this song will make a connection. It does when I play it live. That's just a statement that God can separate us from our sins. That's a hard thing to hold on to, but it's true. It's amazing. I knew that this one had really come from God. Usually, I'm very hesitant to blame any songs on God! I believe He gives us ideas and we are then responsible to turn them into songs, and that's exactly what happened. I knew on that song that God had truly said, "I'm going to give you something here that's good."

Before "Butterfly Kisses" was a single, before anyone knew what success lay ahead for him, Bob Carlisle told us the story of what inspired him to write this song.

Bob Carlisle

"Butterfly Kisses" is a song I wrote for my daughter. I was up late one night in my office. I have a little studio in my office, and I was doing a thing that I kind of do from time to time, kind of half-praying, half-sitting at a piano, just seeing what God wanted to plant on me. I started thinking. Most of the time my mind wanders to my family and my personal life and the things just in my immediate surroundings. It's what God put me here for.

I started thinking about my daughter. She's 17 years old, and I realized I'm not going to have her here in the house much longer, just a few years and she's out of here. I felt so melancholy thinking about it, and I started flashing back on all the times: her in a little party dress and tap-dancing, pony rides, and her first attempt to cook. Just all the things we shared together.

Now she's this grown-up blur. I don't see much of her. I started feeling, not sad because she's such a wonderful kid and just a blessing in my life, but I started feeling melancholy because I know I'm not going to have her with me much longer in this house.

So I wrote "Butterfly Kisses," which is something we would do. I don't know if a lot of people know what butterfly kisses are. When I started writing the song I thought, *Oh, boy, maybe this was something just my little dysfunctional family did!* But I called around and enough people knew what it was. It's this process of putting one's eyelashes up against another's cheek and fluttering them. It's something we would do every night after prayer when we were tucking the kids in.

I started thinking about that, and then I started crying

and writing, in that order. I didn't stop crying and writing until it was done.

The third verse of "Butterfly Kisses" actually has me marrying my daughter off, which is an artistic projection. She's 17, and I was projecting more until when she is 50. I started thinking about what that must be like for a dad to actually stand there and give his daughter away. What's amazing is I've had so many guys come up to me after concerts who've gone through that process and said, "Man, you nailed it. It's difficult." It was a very emotional song. A lot of tears went into the writing and performing of that song.

I asked Scott and Christine Dente to pick the one song that best exemplifies Out of the Grey. They did and inadvertently gave me a description of what is at the heart of their sound.

Out of the Grey

(Scott Dente, Christine Dente)

Scott: If I had to sum it all up from our heart, what I would call a true Out of the Grey song, knowing Christine's heart and what she wants to say to people, and musically for me where I'm at, I would have to say, "Unfolding" off of *Diamond Days*.

Christine: Scott and I tend to lean toward music with lyrics that aren't obvious the first time around, where the melody is just strange enough to make you turn your head, where the chorus lands very soundly on two feet, and where the message provokes thought and moves the heart.

Scott: Make people go back to the lyric sheet and say, "I think I get it. . . . Oh, now I get it." We really shy away from the sledgehammer approach. It's kind of like a movie: Once you've seen it a couple of times, there's not much reason to watch it again. We want people to come back for another view, another angle. We've always come in the side door, rather than walk right through the front door.

Songwriting is personal business shared publicly. The manner in which we approach any creative endeavor is through the medium of ourselves. Here Rob Frazier explains how personality shapes what we do.

Rob Frazier

I knew I was created to minister in the Christian music environment. That's just who I am. I think that's the gift that God's given me. I don't know if this is too heavy to get into or not, but I feel like every Christian artist needs to evaluate what they do; not necessarily in light of who they are musically, but what their spiritual gifts are. You know, the apostle Paul talks about the fact that each of us who are Christians and have accepted God's call on our lives and have decided to follow Him have been given certain gifts. Some people are good at encouraging others, some people are good in the ministry of helps, some are gifted to teach, some to preach, some to be evangelists, some to exhort. Those are, I really believe, my primary gifts: to encourage Christians and to exhort, which just means to encourage in a strong way, to call people out to become who they are meant to be as Christians. No wonder I write all these songs that encourage and exhort, that's the kind of gifts God has given me. That's probably the biggest revelation I've ever received. It's encouraged me to just express myself as a Christian through the eyes of my spiritual gifts and as a musician as well.

One cannot begin to sum up all that Twila Paris means to Gospel songwriting. Here she lets us in on how she views herself as a writer and where she was when she wrote her classic, "God Is in Control."

Twila Paris

I've been so aware the whole time that I've been writing songs, which I guess is almost twenty years now, that first of all, the ability to write songs is a gift—in my case, an unearned one. I never really worked that hard at the craft, certainly not in the early days. I'm sure it's been honed as I worked at writing songs, but I wasn't one who went out and got books and studied and took all these courses. It was a gift.

And I've always considered each individual song as a gift in itself. There are particular songs that especially ring that way. "Lamb of God" is an example that I've always used. I wrote the song very quickly—that's usually what happens when it's one of those that's just a particular gift.

When I was finished it was like, "Wow, did I write that?" And almost as quickly, "No, I couldn't have." Even after that song was written, and this sometimes happens with other songs as well, even years later I would notice something about it (surprising and unexpected) that just sort of happened in the lyric—a neat thing about it that I didn't plan. I didn't even realize it initially.

Sometimes other people will get meanings out of a song. They'll notice things that I didn't even intend, so you know it's larger than you are.

I've had experiences during the writing process or even when I first finish a song when I'll just weep. Sometimes songs that are years old, like once again "Lamb of God" or some nights when I'm singing "Do I Trust You?" or "The Warrior Is a Child," it just becomes very real to me. I may be performing for thousands of people, but they don't know (or maybe they do), that I'm singing the song very directly to the Lord and that He's speaking something to me and that I'm responding to Him on stage while I'm performing. It's a really neat thing for me. I used to think, *Why does He give me these songs? Why does He give them to me and not someone else?* Early on, I sort of thought: *You know what, He realizes that I'm so dense, that I need to hear these messages over and over.* So He thought, *Well, if I give her these songs then she has to get up and sing them over and over every night. At least she'll hear it once, and it'll remind her of this message she needs to hear so often!*

["God Is in Control"] was absolutely a song that was written because I was grappling with that issue. I didn't sit down and say, "What does the body of Christ need to hear this year?" I mean, that's not really something I do. I was driving along in my truck on my way out to my mom's house. She lives about thirty minutes from me, way out in the country. Something, I don't even remember the particular incident there are so many these days, but something had happened that had me saying, *Good night! What is happening to our world, to our society? Crazy people are running rampant and they're doing all these things.* It was like God just spoke to me as I was driving along, it was like, "Hey, ultimately I have the authority. Yes, I have given people free will, but at the end of the day, I am in control." And I responded, "Oh yeah, thanks."

I just started singing this song as I was driving along, just acappella. I wrote the first half of the chorus on the way to my mom's house, the second half on the way back, and later on finished the verses. But I've said before, had my mom not lived so far out in the country the song probably never would have been written. So I'm glad she did.

One songwriter inspires another. God has dreams for us to touch and dreams for us to reach for and never grasp.

Carolyn Arends

Mark Heard has been such an inspiration to me for years and years. When I first started hearing his songwriting, something just clicked in terms of the way that he expressed himself and what a poet he was. He was just amazing.

He actually came and played a concert at my university. It was the college that my boyfriend, Mark, who eventually became my husband, and I were attending. We got a chance to drive him to and from the airport. So that was really exciting for us. I was shy and embarrassed, but my husband was much more brave and asked Mark Heard,—now this is very confusing because they're both called Mark—but Mark my husband-to-be asked Mark Heard if he could give him just a rough tape of some demos of mine or play it for him. He wanted to play it on the way to the airport. Mark Heard said, "You know what, I'm totally exhausted." He had just done the concert the night before, and he'd been up all night and his wife was about to have a baby any second. So he said, "I just don't feel like I'd be able to concentrate right now, but here is ten bucks, why don't you mail it to me?" Really cool guy!

So we did, and a couple of months after that he called me and said that he had really connected with some of the stuff. He asked me to go into the studio for the first time. That demo had just been done in the basement. I believe it was just guitar and vocals. Mark Heard asked me to go into a studio and put down a few more things so he could hear them. From that point on I caught the studio bug. I was in the studio all the time. So, my husband, Mark, as much as he loves Mark Heard, has always sort of secretly blamed him for the years and years of studio bills we've accrued ever since.

But we just kept in touch with Mark Heard after that and he gave me some really great feedback. We had actually come to the place where we had decided to record together. He was going to produce some sides for me and see what we could create together. We were going to do that in September, but he died that summer before we could do it, which was sad on a lot of bigger levels than me not getting to work with him. But I sure put his CD in the player anytime I need some inspiration.

Bill and Gloria Gaither practically invented contemporary Christian music. Their songs have been recorded by some of the biggest names in music as well as become staples in the church hymnals everywhere. Here Gloria remarks on her greatest thrill as a songwriter.

Gloria Gaither

The excitement is to see a song connect with people. Awards have no comparison to seeing a song connect with human beings. Probably the greatest thrill of all is when people take a song away from you. When you walk into some church someplace when you don't know a soul and you're on the other side of the planet and a congregation stands up and sings a song that started someplace in your gut. They have no idea that you wrote it and you almost forget yourself. That's the greatest thrill. That's more of a thrill than the biggest artists in the world recording your songs. Elvis Presley has recorded one of our songs, also Jimmy Durante, Kate Smith, those kind of people. Is that the greatest thrill? To tell you the truth, the greatest thrill is when people own the song that you have written.

Considering what makes a writer a success, Bill Gaither drives home the motivation that exists behind the act of songwriting.

Bill Gaither

From the very beginning, one of the driving motives for both Gloria and me in our writing was that the gospel had made so much sense in our home; how can we help try to make it make sense *especially to the nonbeliever?* I think we get religious sometimes in our verbiage, but it has no real spiritual impact. We've tried very hard to put theology and the gospel that has changed our lives so radically into words people can understand. I hope they can understand *Loving God, loving each other, making music with my friends.* I hope they can understand, *He touched me, oh He touched me.* We've worked hard at that.

When I pillow my head at night I keep saying, "How can I better put this thing that has changed my life so dramatically in some words that everybody can understand?"

Steve Taylor has won over a great number of fans with his clever lyrics and keen, original views on modern culture. Here's a lesson on how he does it.

Steve Taylor

Writing lyrics is as painful as it could possibly be. There's something about that element of surprise that I try to work into what I do. There's a thread that happens through the Bible with subversive communication. It happened with the prophets in the Old Testament and certainly with Jesus and the way that He told stories. Lots of times they would take you down one path and then take it a hard twist. My favorite example is the prophet Nathan when he confronted David with his sin: He did it by telling him a story. He got David really riled up to the point where David said, "Who is this scum?" He's in trouble. And Nathan points a bony finger at him and says, "You're the man!" Right? So the surprise and the shock—there's a whole thread of that going through the Bible. I think that in writing lyrics, especially lyrics that you satire, you're able to do that to good effect. People may think they know where something's going, then you turn a corner and take them by surprise. Hopefully, there's some process of conviction that happens in there too.

Modern culture. There's so many things to poke fun at in modern culture and so many absurdities to it. Of course there's so much that a Christian has to be able to speak into modern culture that that's the thing that fuels my writing. In fact, if I weren't a Christian I'm sure I wouldn't be a writer because I don't know what I would write about.

Opinions on what "Christian" music ought to sound like vary greatly. Kirk Franklin states his view on reaching people with their own music and his response to those who judge.

Kirk Franklin

I think it's important to try to become all things to all men. I believe in hip-hop and all the other things that especially are affecting my community. The Church unfortunately has missed the relationship between the street and the body of Christ. I hope that, with God's will, I can try to bridge it together. I know I'm going to have some traditional people that are going to look down their noses, but, so?

Kirk Franklin ended his performance at the 1997 Dove Awards declaring, "*No white music, no black music, just God's music.*" He was responding to the separation that exists in record stores between

CDs by white artists and CDs by black artists. I asked Kirk for his vision for Christian music.

> Someday, someday, someday to take all the titles and destroy them. I can be honest and say that I kind of get frustrated when I walk into a Christian bookstore and I see the sign that says, "Black Gospel Music." I have a problem with that. I honestly do, and I'm not ashamed of people knowing that. I believe we're doing God a disservice by doing that. So we have to change that, and somebody has got to be bold enough to say it: To be honest, I have nothing to lose, because I didn't ask to be here. I didn't. I just had a couple of songs!

Some songs deal with specific situations within groups of artists. Here dc Talk discusses how a song so particular to them has principles universal to each of us.

dc Talk

(Michael Tait, Toby McKeehan, Kevin Max)

> **Kevin:** It's important for us to write songs that are steeped in reality, especially songs that have something to do with who we are as individuals. When it's something innerband related it's always kind of special because you take it on the stage with you every night or you take it on the TV with you and you're thinking, *Man, this is really about our problems and our solutions within the band.* I'll let Toby say a little bit about this because he's the one who wrote it [the song "Just Between You and Me"], but we honestly feel like this song is such a great statement to the world. Communication is definitely a major problem in relationships. *I mean, if we could only learn how to make things right before the sun goes down.*

Steven Curtis Chapman at London's Abbey Road Studio.
Photo courtesy of Sparrow Communications Group.

Steven Curtis Chapman working with World Vision.

Greg Long in India with Mission of Mercy.
Photo courtesy of Myrrh Records.

Mark Germehl, Rick Florian, and Billy Smiley of Whiteheart.
Photo courtesy of Turning Point Media Relations.

Margaret Becker
Photo by Matthew Barnes.

Chris Eaton
Photo courtesy of Cadence Communications.

Clockwise from left: Don Donahue, president, Rocketown Records; Britt Hamm, manager, Rocketown Artist Services; Cindy Morgan; and Michael W. Smith.
Photo courtesy of Word Records.

Amy Grant performs at Bluebird Cafe in Nashville, Tennessee.
Photo courtesy of Myrrh Records.

Angie and Debbie Winans
Photo courtesy of Against the Flow Records.

Anointed (left to right): Denise "Nee-C" Walls, Steve Crawford, and Da'dra Crawford Gathouse.
Photo courtesy of Myrrh Records.

Point of Grace (left to right): Terry Jones, Heather Floyd, Denise Jones, and Shelley Breen.

Photo courtesy of Word Records.

Bob Carlisle and daughter, Brooke.

Photo courtesy of Music Square West.

Coppernoll in the studio with Michael Card

Photo courtesy of Music Square West.

Crystal Lewis

Photo courtesy of Myrrh Records.

NewSong's Russ Lee. Also pictured, guitarist Leonard Ahlstrom and Eddie Carswell.

Photo courtesy of Turning Point Media Relations. Photo by Stephen Kohl.

Tammy Trent
Photo courtesy of Lenderink Management.

(Left to right): manager Ray Ware, Coppernoll, Bryan Duncan, and promotional manager Jeff Brown.
Photo courtesy of Music Square West.

Sierra (left to right): Wendy Foy Green, Jennifer Hendrix, Deborah Schnelle.
Photo courtesy of Music Square West.

Erin O'donnell
Photo courtesy of Cadence Communications Group.
Photo by Michael Gomez.

4HIM with Michael W. Smith (left to right): Kirk Sullivan, Andy Chrisman, Michael W. Smith, Marty Magehee, Mark Harris.
Photo courtesy of Benson Music Group.

Toby: Confession, forgiveness, reconciliation, these are terms that are slightly alien to our culture, but they are mandatory for human beings to exist together. It's nice to be able to write a song that's based on a principle of God, but the whole world can relate to it. It's not a denominational battle about confession, forgiveness, and reconciliation. Everybody pretty much agrees with those principles, and we need them as human beings. I love those kind of songs where you take something that everyone understands, everyone relates to, but really inside my heart I'm like, *Oh yeah, this is a principle of God, and I'm sprinkling it in my music.*

Christian songwriters are here to serve the Church. I asked Rhonda Gunn how Gospel music can best do just that.

Rhonda Gunn

The greatest way to stay true is to make sure our lyrics as songwriters and the songs that we choose to sing, do in fact minister the gospel of Jesus Christ. We can't forget that it's only the gospel of Jesus Christ that saves souls. It's not how pretty we sing or that we get to minister to people through Christian songs. If we're not mindful of the lyric, making sure that it's understood and that it is the truth, then we're not serving the Church. We're not best serving the kingdom of God as well as we should.

A poetic lyric by comedian Mark Lowry was the start of an unlikely song that has since become an undeniable Christmas classic.

Buddy Greene

"Mary, Did You Know" was an unlikely song because Mark Lowry, who wrote the words, is best known as a

Christian comedian. It was three or four years ago when he handed me this lyric. I knew that he was a singer and songwriter and all these other things, but I think I'd just kind of written him off as a novelty songwriter. You know, he wrote funny songs for his act and everything. But he hands me this lyric that was very thoughtful and beautiful. It's poetry, just what he had to say. It was: "Mary, did you know?" He kept asking this question over and over in the song: Mary, did you know that your son will do this, that he will be this? There are wonderful lines in it like *"This child that you delivered will soon deliver you."* It arrested me right away. *Boy, he's written something pretty significant here.* I finally sat down one night to work on it and within thirty minutes the music was written. It just flowed out of me. I called Mark up and said, "Hey, listen to this!" and played it over the phone. He said, "Mike English is looking for songs; let's get it to him!" So we made a boombox demo of it the next day, and he took it over there. Brown and the rest of them listened to it. It ended up being on the album, and I think it was their first single. It has since just really had a life of its own.

Another interesting thing about it is that it is a song that I've played for non-Christians, and it has a very arresting quality for them too. I don't think it threatens them even though it says probably the strongest things about Christ that a song could say. It is very unashamedly putting Him forth as *the Messiah, the Son of God, the Savior of the World.* These things that usually make Christ an offense, somehow in this song, I don't know if it's the packaging of it or the artfulness of the lyric or whatever, but somehow it makes the person who might be offended by having this message preached at them stop and listen and say, "Wow, that's powerful."

As cowriter with Steven Curtis Chapman or on his own artist Geoff Moore excels as both a writer of driving Rock songs and unfeigned ballads. I asked him if one was easier than the other to write and if his approach was different.

Geoff Moore

Ballads are easier to write. I don't know why. I think it's because the music is more open and you can do more melodically, so you just have a lot more options. In writing Rock music, the challenge there is that it can all sound the same unless you're really clever with the approach to the music and to the melody. And I would just as soon not do anything that someone else has done. So I've probably put a little more work into the Rock side of it, but it's very natural changing hats. Subject matter most of the time does it. When I get an idea for a song it almost always strikes me as whether it's a Rock idea or a ballad idea or somewhere in the middle. The whole idea would also be that what makes a Rock song a Rock song doesn't necessarily have to do with the volume of the drums. It's more of an attitude and an approach to the lyric. I think they're just all part of the kind of music that God intends me to create.

This songwriting tale has all the elements of a great story: a hero, his self-sacrifice, victory though a daughter's love, and God's hand in bringing unlikely events to pass.

Cindy Morgan

My dad had always wanted to be a songwriter when I was a little girl. He made a trip down to Nashville way back about twenty-five years ago. He realized you can't really be a songwriter in Country music unless you're going to live in Nashville. Up to a certain point, you just have to be here. So he gave it all up, and he was a Volkswagen mechanic for as long as I can remember growing up.

When I was looking for songs for *Listen,* I found this old cassette of my mom singing this song and my dad playing guitar. It was a song he had written when I was a little girl that I never had forgotten. I always thought it was such a great lyric. I just thought it was so simple and so profound. So I took those lyrics and Drew Ramsey, who plays guitar for me, and I got together and wrote new music to my dad's words. It was "Listen," and it became the title of the record, the title of the tour, and my dad's first cut. It was so exciting. We kept it a secret from him for three months while we were recording and marketing the record and all the stuff before it came out.

There was a concert in Knoxville, Tennessee. We set it up so they would go out and get him after the song was over. And I'd been telling this story on tour for a month, on the *Listen* tour, so half the country knew about my dad's song. Thirty-nine members of my family were there and my dad. He was the only one in the audience that didn't know what was going to happen. I'd done all this TV stuff and told all this press in Knoxville to tell everybody what was going to happen.

I guess my dad was a nervous wreck because he could just feel something was going on. He just didn't know what. So I got up there and I started telling the story, and I just broke down! And I just couldn't do it, and I was looking at the band saying, "*I can't do it!*" They were saying, "*You have to do it!*" So I cried my whole way through the story about him giving up his dreams. I had to pretend that he wasn't there because I couldn't have made it through. I was so emotional about the whole thing.

Finally, we did the song and my dad got a standing ovation. They brought my dad up and he didn't know what to do. Everybody's just crying. There wasn't a dry eye in the house. It was so emotional, such a great moment. We hugged and we presented him with this plaque. Because of all the lights, he couldn't see up there. So after the presentation was over he said, *"Is it over? I can't see a thing."* Anyway, it was just awesome. It's been great how the single did, and my dad's got a number one plaque at home and that's really fun for him.

Here Cindy sums up, for herself, what it's all about.

The songs are just kind of secondary to what happens with your walk with God. I want to serve God, and I think the best way we serve God is to serve people. I want to be a servant of man, so I can be a servant of God.

I asked the late Rich Mullins to think back to when he first started recording, and if he ever thought one day they would release an album of his greatest hits.

Rich Mullins

Well, some days I did and some days I didn't. There were times when I would say, "Wow, this is a great song" and other times I'd say, "Wow, nobody is going to get this."

I got a great lesson in humility. It was after my first album came out—an album that nobody bought and that no one would play on the radio. I've always been a little arrogant about my own work. I'm kind of a fan of my own. I really do like my own music. I know that upsets people because they think I should be more humble. But it would be ridiculous for me to go to all the bother to write a song that I didn't like. So I'm not going to pretend, saying "Oh gee, I don't know . . ." I really like my songs. I don't know if they're great songs, but I know I really like them.

But I was saying, "Wow, no one bought this album? What's wrong?" I thought, *Gee, I'm going to start writing really cool stuff instead of trying to say what is really important.* About the time that my album had totally bombed and we were starting to work on the second album, and I was getting really serious about picking out songs, a friend of mine shot himself in the stomach. I finally figured out what this song was about. I'd been playing this song for a long time. Generally, I write the accompaniment first and then you just drop a melody over the accompaniment so that it hangs nice. My thing with lyrics is that lyrics are sort of like subtitles. You tell people who might not figure out what the song is about without the help of lyrics. Suddenly I realized this song is not for any record, this song is for this friend of mine. Fortunately, he wasn't very accurate about the way he shot himself, and he lived. But I thought, *I've got to say something to him*, and that's when I wrote "You're on the Verge of a Miracle."

Then, ironically, that became the first song the radio people started playing in heavy rotation. A lot of people will still talk about, "Wow, that was your first radio success" or "That was your first song that went to number one." For me, that song is always a song that I wrote for this friend of mine who was in such a state of darkness, and all I wanted to say to him was hang on because the light can break through.

After the success of that particular song, I felt somewhat ashamed for having thought about how I could write something very popular. What I began to suspect was that there were a lot of people who needed to know that they were on the verge of a miracle, a lot of people who needed to hear about the other side of the world. I can just about go down the list of titles [on *Songs*] and say, "Oh, I remember why I wrote that song. It was for this person in response to this situation."

One thing we all think is that our lives are so unique and so bizarre that no one else could possibly enter into them. Sometimes artists like to be a little off the wall, because as an artist you want people's attention, and shock is one way of getting that attention. But C. S. Lewis said, and I've come to expect that it's very true, that the thing that is common is the thing that is most like art. When a writer, when a painter, when a musician is able to take the thing that you've always suspected and give it words, then you respond to it. This is very Tolstoyan, too, so C. S. Lewis wasn't all by himself in this kind of thinking. I've been pretty much all around the world, and no matter where you're at they respond pretty much the same.

At the deepest level all we need to know is that there really is a God and that He really is good and that He does love us and that we are accepted by Him, that we can be forgiven. Those things are very important to people everywhere. People sometimes make a big deal that I've never done the crossover thing, which, the truth is, I haven't been in love in so many years that I don't think I could write a very good love song.

But then once again, I think there's nowhere my selfishness is more visible than in the way I write. This album [*Songs*] represents ten years of work in the music industry. Someday we'll be called to give an account and I don't think our crown will be the music we wrote; I don't think our crown will be the words we wrote; I think it will be how we have built up the body of Christ, how we have torn down walls of suspicion and walls of fear, how we have shed light on false doctrines, how we've been encouraging truth and how that affects lives, and how we made Jesus visible.

I've never been tempted to write about stuff that I didn't think would help us, because I do believe someday I will die and there will be a judgment. I'm not afraid necessarily of going to hell. I don't think God would have gone to the lengths that He went to forgive me if He were just going to condemn me in the end. Jesus talked of judgment as a matter of what we do with our lives: Did we visit those in prison, did we give to the poor? You know I used to think it was for the advantage of the people in jail and for those people who were naked and hungry. Now I think that He asks us to do that not so that they can be saved, but so we can be. If we want to meet Jesus it won't likely be at church, although I'm a big believer in going to church. I think that when we meet Christ it will be somewhere outside the camp. It will be where people have been marginalized, people who have been literally imprisoned. We will meet Him where we least expect to.

Songwriting is telling what's going on inside the soul of the writer. Hearing and reacting to their songs exposes what's going on inside of us. In the next chapter we'll look at what happens when listeners interact with contemporary Christian music.

6 LIFE IS A DANCE

"In music's sweet harmony, I have all the proof I need of God."

Pat Conroy, "Beach Music"

WHAT IS IT ABOUT GOOD MUSIC that is so easy to identify?

Make a list of your favorite songs of all time and though they may seem very different stylistically they'll have something in common: They move us. Sure the dogs barking "Jingle Bells" is cute, and I grant you that tunes about cool cars and surfin' sound great (especially when played really loud), but if you have ever felt passionately about a song, it has found a place deep inside you. Music does that.

When you combine music with lyrics filled with the Holy Spirit, as the artists in this chapter will profess, something wonderful occurs. A connection is made between artist, listener, and God. That's pretty cool.

There's power in the Word, in teaching, and in encouragement of others. There's unmistakable value in involving ourselves deeply with other Christians. Songs speak to inner core realities of our lives. Like private notes passed from one student to another, they come to us as intimate communications between two people connecting their selves, their experiences, passions, and caring.

In between bands at a concert in Nashville, the dc Talk song "Jesus Freak" came over the sound system in the hall. The mostly teenage crowd with a few parents and pastors started singing along with the song. They knew every word. A year later, I remember just a little about the bands, but I can't forget seeing two generations of Christians feeling solidarity brought on by a song about staying true to our faith in spite of the risk of social ostracism.

Music resets our emotions to the pace, tone, and character of the composition. When combined with lyrics, music opens a window into our souls. It carries into us a message of life on the breeze of melody, harmony, and rhythm. It connects us in an enriching manner, making us feel that we are not alone. But let's not entirely give all the credit to the notes, scales, and key signatures. Music is like an envelope; but it's the love letter inside we tear it up to get to.

Phillips, Craig, & Dean

(Randy Phillips, Shawn Craig, Dan Dean)

Shawn: It's a biblical principle. You look in the Old Testament, and you see where Saul says he actually had an "evil spirit" tormenting him, so they called for David. David played his harp and just ministered to the Lord, and the evil spirit departed. That shows you the power of music. Music is a tool in itself, even beyond the words.

Dan: It's disarming too. You can say something without music and it might offend. But if you put it with music, people just seem to let down their guard a little bit when they hear it. When I first started the group, my dad said, "You'll have a far more effective ministry singing than I ever will preaching because music can go places the spoken word can't go."

Randy: It's a vehicle to the heart.

Songs can bring healing on many different levels. It unlocks our past, and it joins us in our secret places. I can never get through this story from Amy Grant without feeling pain, anger, and sadness. Yet, not contradictory, I am filled with a quiet sense of comfort that comes from sharing our struggles and knowing someone is there.

Amy Grant

A friend and I took a walk one day, and we were talking about one thing and another, and the sun went down. There's something about darkness that makes conversation get a lot more vulnerable. You can't see the other person's face, so there's kind of a balance of vulnerability there. Anyway, I don't know why she chose me, but she started telling me about her experience as a little girl with three different men. One was an uncle, one was a neighbor, and one was somebody else, not her father. Three people in her life who for a period of ten years were sexually abusing her.

The way we talked about it there was a lot of silence. She said, "I can't tell you how alone it makes you feel when your whole life you've got this part of your life that no one even knows exists. So when you're in normal situations you're on tilt on the inside so you're always just trying to level out. You're trying to get the bubble somewhere in the middle." I'm just sitting there thinking about the details of "What does that mean, what does that mean?!" And she said, "I used to spend the night at my grandmother's house. I remember that there was a bathroom that connected my room to my uncle's room. I remember lying in bed at night, so afraid of hearing the floor creak and what that meant." And I said, "Didn't anybody ever know?" And she said, "No, nobody ever knew." And I asked, "Didn't anybody ever see?" And she said, "One time I was on a screened-in porch, and my brother came up and saw my uncle and me on the porch." I didn't ask the details of what was going on, but I asked, "What happened?" And she said, "We locked eyes, my brother and I." And I said, "What did you say?" And she said, "Oh, Amy, I'd already disappeared by then."

She talked about the smell of nicotine on fingers and how that still nauseates her today.

Well, we talked and talked and talked. I came home, and I have a little girl. I woke up in the middle of the night, just sweating and crying. I couldn't get away from it. Because this was not [abuse from] her daddy, these were just people exposed to her.

It happened again the next night and the third night. Finally I just said, "I'm going down to the basement, and I'll come out when I can." I was down there for hours. I paced that floor, and I screamed. I railed at God and I railed at life and at that son of a gun, all three of them that would do that to a child. And I wrote that song ["Ask Me"].

I think I related to it because in completely different circumstances I knew what it felt like to be manipulated. We all know what it feels like to be a part of someone else's agenda. Even as a adult, in your own naiveté you play into someone else's plan and wind up someplace you never intended to be. Abuse is something that everyone knows on some level, either because you were the recipient of it or because you initiated it.

I wrote it and demoed it and I was going to give it to this friend of mine as a gift. This room was arranged a little differently, but we had the stereo in that room and the speakers were up there. I said, "Hang on just a second, I'm going to try to make this sound okay." She was sitting in the middle of that sofa. I'm in the other room adjusting the treble and the bass, and I don't really know what I'm doing to her emotionally. I hadn't really considered it; it was just my gift to her.

We started the song and when I came back into the room, I was facing her back and all I could see was her shoulders just racked; she was sobbing. *I felt so awful,* and I didn't know what I'd done. All I did was just slip behind her in the sofa and put my arms around her. The song finished. She cried and I held her, and I was just getting ready to apologize, because I felt like I had gone somewhere that I was not invited to go and been so presumptuous to write about it and even more so to play her the song. With my apology just poised on the tip of my tongue, she said, *"How did you know? How did you know how it felt?"* I did. I knew how she felt. For a little bit. I don't know why I did, but I did.

I wound up putting it on the record because she asked me to. The wild thing about doing that song is, you know we talked about how music connects people. A lot of women have that in their past—a lot of men too. But what I love more than anything is playing that song, which is, I think, done in a very respectful way toward the people involved; I mean it doesn't say anything really overtly nasty or humiliating. But I don't ever do that song in concert that I don't see people standing up, solitary figures one at a time all over the auditorium, certainly what I can see in the wash of the stage lights. And always, I don't know, it feels like their own opportunity to stand up and say, "I'm not alone" or "This is my story" or "I'm a survivor." Music is a powerful thing. It does connect us to who we are.

In the unplanned, unexpected moments of life, God can take the everyday and make it life-changing. Maybe it's just the interaction that takes place when someone describes to an audience why the songs are written. Maybe it's the exposure to God's Spirit in the music that opens ears. My suspicion is that this reaction happens more often than is reported.

Stephen Curtis Chapman

A lady stood in line and came through as I was at a bookstore signing some of my records. She said she had heard me at a totally unrelated event, a Wal-Mart convention. I was singing for their salespeople, invited in as one of the musicians whose music they sell. It wasn't in a Christian music context at all, I just played my songs and told why I write the songs that I do.

This lady came through and said just something had impressed her. She'd never heard me before but liked the music. So she got one of my CDs as a result of that night and started listening to it back and forth to work in her car. She said she found herself one day just weeping and pulling her car over. She couldn't understand why every time she listened to this music there was this huge hunger and emptiness inside of her. She began to realize, "I don't have what this music is celebrating and talking about." She said, "That began my journey toward coming to realize my need for a relationship with Jesus Christ."

That was one of those things. Even in unplanned, unexpected ways, God can take and use anything that we do for His glory.

Songs from the heart touch hearts of different people in a variety of walks of life. Bob Carlisle had no intention beyond putting his emotions about his daughter into a song. He didn't fully realize that his feelings written into a song while his family slept would later resonate with millions of people he would never meet in person.

Bob Carlisle

When we released the album *Shades of Grace,* the album was doing very well in the Christian marketplace. It was selling well, staying in the top twenty sales, and that was really gratifying for me because I'm at a place in my life where I'm trying to be even more transparent with my music and about my life as a solo artist. It told me that folks were actually listening to the music and were taking a lot of the things I was singing and saying to heart. But no one had any idea that what happened would happen.

The song "Butterfly Kisses" crossed over into mainstream radio without us even trying. It wasn't something we set out to do at all. It was one of those things that I thought only happened in the 1950s: a program director who had a daughter somehow got a copy of the song. He listened to it, and it really affected him emotionally. So he decided to take a chance and play the record late at night, and then his phone lines jammed for half a day. It was one of those things. It was a real head-scratcher. It was just word of mouth. The song's popularity really just spread like a brush fire, to the place where the song is at the top of the pop charts. Pretty amazing.

The song was actually not intended to be released by me or anybody else necessarily. It was a very emotional song, a very personal song for me. I wrote the song, and later brought in my friend Randy Thomas, a songwriter and a dear friend of mine, to help me cross the Ts and dot the Is and really make it the song that it is. But we weren't even intending to release it on the album. When it came time to select songs for the *Shades of Grace* album, my wife *strong-armed* me into playing "Butterfly Kisses" for the record company guys that came to my home to listen to music. I was reluctant to do so because it was such an intensely personal song, but I played it for them and they really loved it and everyone wanted it on the album. So we put it on.

None of us had any idea that people would take it to heart the way they have. I mean, it's just been amazing. I think it speaks to the fact that people are hungry for something like this.

I do a lot of interviews with secular radio stations, and they ask me if I have a platform of some kind that I'm using with this song, and I tell them absolutely not. I'm not trying to cram values down anybody's throat. I'm not trying to stand up and represent what perfect fatherhood is supposed to be like. I wrote this song for my kid, and I'm not perfect. "*With all that I've done wrong, I must have done something right.*" It's not a song about being a great father, it's a song about being a grateful man. I think *that's* what people are relating to across the board, whether it be Christian or secular venues. They're relating to the fact we're all just goofy, trying to make it from Monday to Tuesday, but despite ourselves, God has chosen to give us these little bundles of innocence to be responsible for. It's just very touching.

The song "Butterfly Kisses" has allowed me to capture a vision of this country that I didn't have before. I've been able to see, just as an ambassador, this song open people's hearts before I even get there. I was received so warmly by the folks at *Oprah Winfrey*, *The Tonight Show,* and *Good Morning America.* Spencer Christian, the weatherman on *Good Morning America,* for example, embraced me because he has daughters. He told me how the song had meant so much to him before he even met me, before I even sang the thing.

The idea that this country has embraced the song the way they have reminds my old, cynical, jaded heart that there is an enormous heart in this nation. This song has apparently pierced that heart. The idea that Bob Carlisle and Spice Girls are jockeying for the top slot in *Billboard's* record charts is not because we're jockeying for the same audience. There's a sleeping giant heart in America that has just been awakened by this song.

A sleeping giant. More than two million people have walked into record stores to get a copy of "Butterfly Kisses." It wasn't a hooky title, a great lyric, or a memorable melody that awakened that giant (although the song has all three), it was a message of fatherly gratitude, not intented for public consumption, that connected us, one person at a time.

In isolation, away from the love of God and others is where darkness seeks to triumph. Here Christian music and radio team up to share hope in Christ through a song called, "Where There Is Faith."

4 HIM

(Marty Magehee, Kirk Sullivan, Andy Chrisman, Mark Harris)

Andy: A guy in Dallas who had been at the end of his rope decided to end it all. He had a bottle of sleeping pills and just swallowed the whole bottle. He turned on his radio to get his mind off of what was about to happen to him and found the Christian station there in Dallas. "Where There Is Faith" came on the radio. He said as he listened to the words he began to weep and realized what he did was wrong. He said he still doesn't know how, but he began to cough up the pills to the point that they weren't lethal anymore. He found someone that he knew who was a Christian and that person led him to the Lord that night.

It was neat for him to come and share. He said, "You guys are the reason I'm alive because of what you sang in your music." You can't put a price tag on that. When God uses you in those ways it's incredibly humbling.

Marty: I've had several people come up to me who were healed at our concert during "Where There Is Faith." Most of them were people who had arthritis and that kind of thing. One woman specifically said that after the song was over, she felt no pain in her knees. She got off her chair and kneeled all the way down and she was fine. God had healed her. Those sort of things happen. We have the salvation experiences, the restorations, and the inner healings. But then to actually have physical healings, that's a blatant, token sign of God's hand and His anointing.

In concert, on CD and tape, and on the radio, music filled with the Spirit of God is powerful. A community gathered together for a common purpose has that kind of power. That's what Larnelle Harris sees in the artists performing contemporary Christian music.

Larnelle Harris

I still have the same ulterior motive that I've always had: writing and singing songs that are going to challenge people and bring them closer to the Lord. That's always been my agenda. It's good to be part of a team effort, because that's what's going to make this happen.

I get so tired of hearing about something being boring or something not being liked. If you spend three minutes in that auditorium with all of these different kinds of music going on and the Lord really using them all well, it doesn't take long to understand that Clay [Crosse] and I and all the rest of us are part of a team. That team is substantiated and undergirded by the Church and by the Spirit of the Lord. If it's not, then it doesn't have any business up here. My purpose in this first record with Brentwood, which I'm just so excited about, has not changed. As I sat in the auditorium tonight [at the 1997 Dove Awards] I saw that something else hadn't changed: We are still a team, and the Lord is using this package and all of you in one way or another to further His cause.

The enthusiasm of teenager Jaci Velasquez is contagious. Her message that we can uplift and support each other through everyday problems, however, isn't to be disregarded as youthful verve. Here she addresses sexual purity, but the strengths to be found in one another should be an encouragement to us all.

Jaci Velasquez

The reason "The Promise" is hitting well with a lot of young people, like me, is because I am 16. I have the same exact temptations that they do. I deal with the same things every day. I have those same problems. If we can all just get together and make this promise, and really have a unity, we can make a difference. We can do all these things if we'll just do it together.

I have a friend who is 14. She just had a baby, and she and her baby have full-blown AIDS. Think about that. Put yourself in that situation. I don't know what in the world I would do. But I do know there's only one way to fix this. We can't do anything about this situation now—all we can do is pray. But the way we can fix this in the future is to make that promise and keep ourselves pure before God.

Ron Kenoly is first and foremost a praise and worship leader. Here he lets us know his identity and goal for his music ministry. He speaks of the design of God's music to be useful for the Church.

Ron Kenoly

I think what's important is that the public or the Christian community recognize that the music that we do is first designed for the Church: to help the pastors and the local churches reach a higher level in their worship experiences. That is our first goal. So a lot of the music that we do will not necessarily be designed for the radio or for entertainment purposes. Our main goal is to bring people into the manifest presence of the Lord Jesus Christ. That's our main objective; that's our main goal.

I know that in my own heart I've tried deliberately to present myself and my identity to be synonymous with praise and worship. I don't necessarily consider myself a Christian artist; I'm a praise and worship leader.

All the other things that happen in our lives are God's way of rewarding us in this life for being faithful to the call He placed on our lives. But we don't necessarily do music to get on the charts or be heard on the radio. We do the music so that the Church that Jesus Christ established can realize a higher level in their worship experience.

The Newsboys gave an example of what they see in their concerts regarding their music making an impact. They remind us that it's effortless sometimes forgetting the power of God even when you're standing in the middle of it.

The Newsboys

(John James, Jeff Frankenstein, Peter Furler, Jody Davis, Duncan Phillips, Phil Joel)

John: A good example of music reaching people is the show we did in Salt Lake City. A lot of those kids who came there had never been to a concert before, let alone a Christian concert. And just the number of comments that we had was just unbelievable! It was obvious that the music and the message had really affected their lives. Jeff and I were just sitting there afterward, and we realized that these kids were the same kids that a lot of the time the church is trying so hard to reach, and yet music is able to reach out and touch their lives. It really encouraged me.

Sometimes you do what you do five, six nights a week, and you get into a routine of doing what you do. Sometimes it's good to step out of the circle and really see through other people's eyes the impact that your music can have. I don't think you always realize exactly how much impact your music can have. It really challenged me.

Jeff: Salt Lake City is about 90 percent Mormon. It was the first Christian concert they'd had there in ten years. All the Christian youth pastors in that whole city totally bonded together and just brought out about 5,000 people, which was unheard of for the area. John and I went out after the show to talk to people, and it just blew us away! One after another came up and thanked us for coming, "Nobody ever comes up here. Bands just don't want to come up here to play." There were something like 1,300 decisions for Christ. It was just unbelievable. Sometimes you don't realize what it's doing, but that really touched us.

Christian music is the only style of music defined by its lyrical content. I asked Steve Taylor what all the different Christian artists who play Rock, Rap, Southern Gospel, and Pop have in common.

Steve Taylor

We all use a lot of the same notes in the scale. A lot of songs are in 4/4 time. We use some of the same prepositions in our lyrics and things like that, so we've got that going for us.

Well, one of the cool things about Christian music is it's the only genre of music that's based on what the lyrics are talking about. From that standpoint, you could put any of the artists together in the same room and we've got something to talk about because we all share the same faith. One of the cool things about Gospel music is we all have the same backstop.

In this story a 15-year-old girl teaches John Elefante a lesson about the power of Christian music.

John Elefante

The most impacting story for me was a girl who wasn't contemplating suicide, *she was going to commit suicide.* I had the privilege of meeting her back at Cornerstone about five years ago. She was a 15-year-old girl who was about to take her life when she heard a Mastodon song called "Life on the Line" and decided not to take her life. She wrote me a letter and it just about laid me out. If that's not power through Christian music, then Christian music doesn't have any power.

Here's another story of a young girl whose heart and life were saved through the message presented in a song.

East to West

(Patrick Neal Coomer, Jay DeMarcus)

Neal: It's great at the end of the night to see people make commitments to Christ and people drawn closer to the Lord. We had a situation where a girl came up to us after a concert and said, "If it weren't for your song 'Fearless Heart' I wouldn't be alive today." She was literally writing her suicide note at the moment when that song came on the radio, and the Lord used that song at that moment to just turn her life around. So two weeks later, here is this girl at the concert, and she's standing there telling you that. She also brought a friend with her. Her friend was unsaved, but she also made a commitment to Christ that night.

The difference in the music we sing. It carries a message of hope and encouragement maybe that they wouldn't hear on 97 Rock. There's more than good music to what we sing about. *Time* magazine did a cover story that asked, *"Are Music and Movies killing America's Soul?"* What we have is the alternative. I hope in the future Christian music will become the true alternative music. People will say, "Okay, here's something that's more positive. It has hope."

In an interview, you're never sure which questions will prompt the most interest in the interviewees. When I asked Billy and Sarah Gaines if Christian music makes any difference, they spoke passionately about the difference it's made not only in the lives of fans, but in themselves as well.

Billy & Sarah Gaines

Sarah: Oh yes! I was saved listening to Andrae Crouch's "In Remembrance."

Billy: Both of us believe so strongly in the power of music. It's just the way that God would have it that both of us came to the Lord listening to music. I was 14 years old when my cousin witnessed to me and I really understood the concepts. But man, one day I was lying on my sofa—my mom had a Kate Smith record of all things. I was listening to the song "There Is Room at the Cross for You." The lyrics of that song just got me, and I really understood. *"Though millions have come, there's still room for one, there's room at the cross for you."*

It was right there that the message just finally settled in on me. I believe that if someone had been just reciting those words, it wouldn't have had the same impact as someone who was singing them. So I believe so strongly, *so strongly*, in music making a difference.

A number of people have told me that they've heard one of our songs on the radio and they had to pull over to the side of the road to just praise God or to cry. That kind of response is not an everyday thing; it's not an everyday situation that you're driving down the street and somebody just says something on the radio and you want to pull over. And to think that they're so affected by the music that they pull over to rejoice in the Lord or just weep because God spoke to them in a deep way, that's powerful.

So, *I know*, as long as the Word is in the music, it has power. If the music doesn't have the Word, though, it really doesn't have any power. If you've just got music there, the music will always stir some kind of emotion. I can listen to jazz and get moved by it. But when you put the Word of God, or not necessarily direct Scripture, but when you put the principles of the Word of God into music, it is a powerful, powerful instrument.

Billy still remembers the words from a Kate Smith song many years later. He remembers how he felt hearing that song. The source of meaning is our Lord and Savior, Jesus Christ. His gospel is articulated through lyrics, and its emotion is shaped by His invention, music. It helped shape the careers of Billy & Sarah Gaines and another artist named Paul Q-Pek.

Paul Q-Pek

When I was about 14 and starting to go to high school, I became exposed to contemporary Christian music for the first time. I was just blown away by it, I loved it and wanted to hear more and find out more about it. I started buying all these different artists' tapes. The first contemporary

Christian music I ever heard was The Imperials. I think the album was called *Sail On.* It was the first album that Russ Taff was on. I just couldn't believe it was Christian music. I thought, *This is great!* because I loved contemporary sounding music, but I was always told that the words are bad and that rock and roll was bad because it glorifies evil things. But I loved that style of music. So when I heard this contemporary Christian music for the first time I thought it was wonderful. I thought, *This is what I need to be doing.*

We think of Christian music as having its greatest impact on teens and college-age people. Here the classic quartet The Imperials share the impact they have seen in prisons among society's toughest men.

The Imperials
(Armond Morales, David Will, Jeff Walker, Steve Ferguson)

Steve: We were in a maximum security prison about two months ago for a service. There were about 900 men and they were obviously pretty rough-looking characters. We just began to minister. At first they weren't very receptive, but as we went on, several of them began to worship the Lord, lifting their hands and standing. I know the other men would tell you this, but I sensed the Spirit of the Lord just begin to soften the hearts of those hard guys. By the end of the service, I'm not sure the exact count, but I think there were a hundred or so men who gave their hearts to the Lord for the first time.

So music is effective, but without the message and the anointing of the Spirit of the Lord, music just isn't enough. It just doesn't have the bang for the buck.

David: There's another thing that music does that the spoken word or even preaching can't do: It's the repetition and the melody [that make a message memorable]. Mike Perky told me once that he preached the same sermon three Sundays in a row, the same message, and on the third Sunday he had one lady come up after and ask if he had ever preached this before. He said he discovered that people can't remember more than three points in a sermon. But a song is something that you can wake up with. The melody plays over and over again. The music speaks to the heart and the words speak to the spirit person on the inside. That's why it's so important that the words and melody go together to make that message stick in the spirit. That's what's powerful about music.

Part of what's wrong today is that kids are getting the wrong messages, and they're hammering away the wrong things into their spirits. If you have a song going on inside you all day about killing a cop, eventually somebody's going to do that. The world doesn't understand that. They don't understand how powerful music is.

God uses whatever and whomever He desires to reach people. When Shirley Caesar ends her story with, "a great voice, a great voice," I'm not sure if she means a singer or an instrument of God.

Shirley Caesar

Let me say this: Even though I am a Gospel singer, I certainly thank God for allowing me the privilege last year on the Grammys to sing with Whitney Houston [where Gospel music could be heard by many]. I sang one of my own songs, "Heaven," but it was Whitney Houston [who made it happen], please believe me! God will use whatever vehicle He chooses to use to get this gospel of Jesus Christ across. And God used her to catapult me to where I'm standing right now. So I just thank God for the wonderful and awesome privilege of singing with Whitney Houston. A great voice, a great voice.

We are humbled that God would choose any of us for service, but He does. The women of Sierra tell two stories about people: one at the end of life, the other beginning a new one.

Sierra

(Wendy Foy Green, Deborah Schnelle, Jennifer Hendrix)

Wendy: In all humility I want to say it's unbelievable how God has used our music. We say that in humility because we have people come up and we could sit and tell you story after story about the way that people have been touched by our music.

For instance, just last week at a concert in Houston, a lady came up and said, "My husband passed away. Your music was our favorite music and we would listen to your songs over and over and over. It was his favorite music. He died of a sudden aneurysm. We had no idea beforehand. When he was cremated, I went up and spread his ashes while the song "Sierra" played because that has touched us in a way that no other music had." And you just think, *Okay, God. That is the most humbling thing I've ever heard.*

We know people are listening to our music and being impacted. We don't know why God chose us three regular, goofy girls, but we hear story after story. Another guy came to our concert in Oregon and said, "I could not get my granddaughter to listen to Christian music." She was living a little bit wild. He said, "I took her to see you in concert, and it was the first Christian tape she bought. She listens to it all the time." She came to see us in concert, and it's changed her life.

We don't know why God chose us for that, but we're so thankful that He chose someone to bring her to Him. At that concert three people came to know Christ. I know that God is allowing people to be impacted by the music that He's given us. It is very humbling for us.

People are reached into by the message in the music and by the gift of a CD or tape. Here Al Denson gives both.

Al Denson

I met a man who runs this company I had been working with. He's not a Christian, and his mouth is not real clean all of the time, but he's one of the greatest guys in the world. You'd love to hang out with the guy. He really cares, he's got a tender heart, and he's just super cool. He just doesn't know the Lord.

I'd given him a CD of *Take Me to the Cross.* I gave one to a bunch of other people; basically I gave one to everybody in that company. I didn't hear another thing from him for three or four weeks. He didn't say a thing about it. Everybody else said, "This is great," and whatever. I was kind of wondering because I'd really done most of that for him. Then all of a sudden he was on this New York trip and came back on a late-night flight. When he got on the plane he opened his briefcase and there's an Al Denson CD. He said, "I'm going to listen to that." So he pulled out the CD player, and he set it up. He said, "I don't want to listen to much of this thing" so he looked at the title and said, "'Take Me to the Cross,' let's find that song. That's probably a good one." So he punched up to five on the CD, and he listened to it.

Now, another friend is flying in the seat across the aisle from him, and he said he saw him do all this. Right in the middle of listening to the CD, the man just starts crying. He had tears in his eyes and he went back and he listened to it four or five times. The next day he calls me (not my friend, but the guy I gave the CD to). He calls me up and said he wanted to tell me how much that song had blessed him, how much that song meant to him and says, "When I got home it was around 2:30 in the morning. I went into the house and my wife woke up and she looked at me and I said, 'I'm just going to see our daughter.'" He has a little 4-year-old daughter, and he picked up his daughter out of the bed and he just held her and said he was sorry. Then he asked me on the telephone, "Can you help me be a better dad to my daughter and show me how I get God in my life so I can be a good godly father to my daughter?" That just blew me away on the phone, and the guys in the office say he's been different.

That's just in the last two weeks. That's the kind of thing where we never know what's going on and we never know how it's going to go. Over the years I've gotten tons of stories, but I believe in telling you what's just happened in the last two weeks.

Music is just a vehicle for carrying a message that glorifies God and serves people. We can't celebrate the gift of music and deny the God who gave it to us. In the next chapter we'll take a look at how the Christian music industry serves the less fortunate in a tangible way, taking faith into action.

7

THE PASSIONS OF THE COMPASSIONATE

"The rewards of compassion are not things to wait for. They are hidden in compassion itself. I know this for sure."

Henri J. M. Nouwen, <u>Here and Now</u>

HAVE YOU EVER WANTED to change the world? I've included simple instructions below on how we can change someone's world and lick apathy in our own hearts in the time it takes to lick a postage stamp.

Who are the compassionate? The compassionate are those who will help out the needy. They may give their time, or money, or prayers to help their fellow men. They show their compassion here in the United States and across the seas in countries all around the world.

Some do it because it serves Christ or because they have empathy for the less fortunate. Some do it because they've decided long ago to do what is right with their lives and they know in their hearts this is right.

Prepare yourself for a joyous ride. This is a chapter filled with good news of another kind.

The hungry are being fed, the naked clothed, the imprisoned visited, the thirsty quenched, and the gospel is being preached. If you have supported any of these causes, you should feel great about it. Why someone who has resources wouldn't support them is beyond comprehension.

Life is confusing. Even understanding God sometimes is hard. But when we give, we are immediately transported to the center of God's will for us: to obey God and to love others. Giving accomplishes both without any theological head-scratching required.

Many very large organizations are running on small donations. Five and ten-dollar checks are common and welcomed by these organizations. Rich Mullins said that he once thought it was for their benefit we gave. He told me that after working within the practice of giving he determined the benefit was much more his own.

Make out a check and send it to one of these groups that will in turn give it to the hungry, naked, imprisoned, and poor. You are assured that the Lord is delighted in your doing this, and that should make you feel great about your value as a human being. The people who benefit by your love in motion have faces and names. They give hugs to their loved ones, they celebrate important events, and they work to make life better. Giving is never wrong. It is always, always, right. Build caring into your monthly routine.

Now that you care, what is it you can do? Is it only $10 per month? Wonderful, because when 100,000 of you give just $10, you've collectively given one million dollars. And one million dollars makes a difference; therefore your small gift makes a difference too. We have determined to tithe 10 percent of all of our business earnings to charities that seek to obey God's instructions in love. When you bought this book, a share of your money moved from your pocket toward God's work. Somewhere in the world tonight a need is being met while you lie in bed reading this. You just made someone's day. Feels good doesn't it? Want to feel even better? Do it one more time! Which charities would the Lord place on your heart right now? Have you ever thought about it?

Greg Long

> I had known for about two days that I was going to get to see Mother Teresa. On the way over there, winding through the streets of Calcutta, all of a sudden I started to freak out. *What am I going to say to her? What am I going*

to say to Mother Teresa? It's hitting me now that we're going to be face to face, and I had no idea what I was going to say. One of the pastors from the mission church who was the contact between Mother Teresa and **Mission of Mercy** said, "Greg, just say what's on your heart."

She walked out in the humblest of ways—no pretense whatsoever—out of one of the humblest of buildings, just cement flooring. It was obvious that she was there for the people. They said, "Mama Teresa, this is Greg Long from the United States. He works with us over at the mission raising awareness and help for the children." She said, "That's fantastic! Do it for the glory of God, Greg. Do it for the glory of God." I said, "Hey, yes ma'am, I just want to tell you what an example you are to myself and everyone in the world of what a Christian should be. I just want to say thank you for being an example." She said, "Oh, it's my privilege to do it. For the glory of God and the good of man we do it all."

As I held on to her hand and looked into her eyes, I thought to myself that this woman could have an audience with anyone in the world. Any world leader at any time. She could call any president, any prime minister, any person of royalty, and they would take the call. And she talked to me. As soon as I was done, there was a poverty-stricken Asian man who had traveled twelve hours by train to ask a blessing for someone in his family. At the mission I was considered this "American recording artist." "He's on television; he has music on the radio." She loved me, but she treated this next guy who was poverty-stricken the very same way: full of love, full of compassion.

I left there with a sense of awe and humility and a kind of a warning to be careful how I treat people. I realized it's all done for the glory of God. If we stacked up all I've done in my life and compared it next to hers, it's mountain and molehill, if even that. So none of us have the right to get puffy about what we do because she's done it all and doesn't take anything for it. We have a tendency to pat ourselves on the back a lot over in this country. She doesn't. I didn't ask her a lot of questions. She prayed for me, that God would be with me in what I do, and I left.

I had dinner with my aunt Donna, my mom's sister, about a week and a half ago. We were playing Skipbo cards and eating dinner. She said, "What was it like meeting Mother Teresa?" I said, "It was like a dream. I met Mother Teresa." It's like I'm living a dream somehow. It's just amazing what God has done. The biggest thing to learn from her, whether you knew her or not, 'cause we all saw what she stood for, is that Christ came for the hurting. If I'll reach out to those who are hurting, God will take care of it. Because you know what? Everybody's going to be hurting at one time or the other. The wealthiest of the wealthy are going to be broken down and hurting and feeling helpless.

I was sitting on a plane with a guy a couple of months ago who was a wealthy businessman. He told me about all the companies he owned—one in Tokyo, one in New York, one in Los Angeles. But his wife had left him six months before. I didn't tell him what I did as far as music, but I told him I went to Bible college and that I'm working in the ministry. When he heard that, boy, he was ready to unload. Here's this wealthy businessman, in his late fifties, talking to me because I'm in the ministry, and all of a sudden I realize that this man's at the end of his rope. He told me, "*I've tried everything I could do to make my wife stay, but I can't make her stay.*" And I realized sometimes that's where God needs to have us, because we rely on ourselves way too much. We have to understand that we can't, but He can.

Every one of us is going to be there. If we'll just give to the hurting, we'll always have someone to minister to.

God will bring them in at that time as we are showing love to them. That's what I learned from Mother Teresa.

Glad

(Chris Davis, Jim Bullard, Ed Nalle, John Gates, Paul Langford)

Ed: The two things that I'm proudest of are the children who have been sponsored via our work with **Compassion International,** which numbers now some 7,000 children. That's a pretty wonderful thing. It's concrete. We can look back and say that it really matters. Second, the people who have come to know the Lord at various concerts over the years. I met a kid in a heavy-metal band here at this convention [Gospel Music Week] who accepted the Lord at one of our concerts twelve years ago. I've met some guys who had accepted the Lord at concerts along the way and now they're youth pastors or pastoring churches. Those kinds of things. When you see that some of the fruit was good fruit and that it lasted, those are the things that really matter. I mean, there are certain songs that you're happy with, you're proud of, you think you did a good job, but beyond that it's the effect that we're going for. It's the ministry that occurs in a person's life as God takes some simple lyric that we dream up or that someone has dreamed up and speaks to somebody in a way that you had not even imagined that He would.

Chris: We've been associated with Compassion International for about ten years. Around 1985 we took a trip to Haiti and it was an extreme eye-opener. The conditions of poverty that existed there were unlike anything that I'd ever seen. I grew up in Europe, but I'd never seen poverty like that. Seeing the work they were doing and the way the funds were being used really convicted us that this was an organization that we could really believe in and endorse in our concerts. Personally, I've been to Haiti, Mexico, and Ecuador. Those are trips that after I'd returned made me question everything I held dear and reassess my value system. They are one of the main reasons Glad does what we do.

Over the years we've been a part of the sponsorship of 7,000 kids. Compassion provides the basic necessities of life, and beyond that, they do it with a Christian perspective. So the kids have clothes and they have food. They also have an education, which in a lot of these countries their leadership doesn't put a premium on.

Point of Grace

(Denise Jones, Shelley Breen, Heather Floyd, Terry Lang)

Terry: Mercy Ministries is a home in Louisiana and Nashville that takes in girls who have become pregnant or have been messing around with drugs or alcohol in a really bad way. They are able to come live in the house free of charge. Twenty girls can stay at a time now. The house in Nashville can hold fifty girls. They take the girls in and they give them skills like cooking and cleaning and give them new clothes and a fresh start. They teach them schoolwork and most of all about the Lord. A lot of girls come in without a clue. They are our ages, so when we see the girls it's always humbling that God spared me from rape or incest or anything that they've gone through. God really does show His mercy on that home. The girls are just wonderful, wonderful girls. We had a song written that is called "The House That Mercy Built." It stands for the home, but it also stands on its own. If you didn't know about Mercy Ministries, you'd know about the love and the mercy of Jesus Christ.

Clay Crosse

On our tour with Jaci Velasquez, we're going to be raising

awareness about **World Vision** in all the cities we go to, trying to get people to sign up to sponsor these children. It's a great organization. It's one of those organizations where you just stand back and look at what they do and realize this is incredibly Christlike. This is what He would want us to do. I'm going to have the opportunity this week to go to Haiti to see some of the work that they do down there and meet some of the children that are being affected by their ministry. I'm looking forward to it. I think it's going to be very emotional and eye-opening to me. I anticipate walking out of there very thankful for what the Lord has done in my life and where He allowed me to be raised and where I grew up. I look at this whole world, and it's pretty amazing when I realize for some reason God allowed me to grow up in America in a Christian home. I don't know why that happened, but I'm thankful for it because there's a lot of poverty, a lot of desolation, and a lot of hopelessness out there.

Through World Vision I'm just trying to do my part to show these children that there is hope through Christ. That's what's great about World Vision—they feed people and give them a chance at an education. They give them shelter and clothing, but through it all they show them that it's about Christ. That's why we're doing it. They always share Christ.

After Clay's mission visit in Haiti, he included this in his report:

I've never seen such poverty in my life. I got the sense that the people there were just on a mission to eat. It was a mission, an opportunity to see what World Vision is doing there. You can read about it or see videos, but when you're actually out there with the people who are benefiting from World Vision, it's great. It motivates you to want to do more.

I wish all the people who give support could have gone with me to see what's going on there.

Haiti is very encouraging. I saw schools that children got to go to. I actually went to their classes and got to spend time with them. These schools wouldn't have been possible without World Vision. I saw clinics in the communities for the people. Which, if they were not there, the people would have to walk twenty or thirty miles to a hospital. I saw business opportunities for them: a corn mill where they bring their corn to be processed. It was set up by World Vision and, from what I could see, it's thriving. These are just things that help a community get on their feet and hopefully one day be self-sufficient. That's the goal. The goal of World Vision is that one day there won't have to be a World Vision.

There are many types of contests. The music industry may use sales and number one songs to determine which artist is on top, but Larnelle Harris has a different kind of contest in mind.

Larnelle Harris

I don't know that Christian music can draw people to Jesus. But as we the Christian artists come together with the pastors that are in their pulpits on Sunday and constantly in the Word, we become a team. You know what kind of contest I want to have if we're going to have one? Hey, Mark [Harris], Marty [Magehee], Pam [Thum], I'll outdo you in doing good! Now if we're going to compete against each other, let's have a [real] contest! Dallas [Holm], the Lord is calling us to do good. You know what, I may not sell more albums or I may sell more, but that's not the issue. The issue is, let's outdo one another in doing good. That's a good contest. It's iron sharpening iron. I want to be on as few pedestals as possible, and I want to be on more prayer lists.

Michael Card

I sense, in a very different way, **The Bible League** and I are doing the same thing. I'm trying to present the Bible to people in America primarily. It's the same ministry, but we each do it in a different way. We're just very much preoccupied with getting people interested in the Bible. I think we're doing the same thing. I think I gain more credibility with having my name associated with them than they do being associated with me.

I've gone out in the field and seen the need out there. When I was in the Philippines I went to this massive warehouse that they have that every four to six months is filled all the way to the roof with Bible study materials and Bibles. Then again, every six months or so it's completely emptied. So I've seen the need. So far, Bibles for China has raised a couple of million dollars. That sounds like a lot, but when you see the need, and when you see the numbers, you're made aware of the need. I just feel the burden for that. I'm not good at asking for money. That's not my thing at all. But I'm pretty unashamed to ask for money for this cause, for the purpose of putting Bibles into the hands of people who want them, who are asking, who are *begging* for them.

Obviously, I think it's important enough to "risk" asking people. People in general, especially Americans, don't like to be asked for money. I don't like to be asked for money, but I do like to know when there's a substantive ministry. If I can't give money to them; maybe I can pray for them.

The Bible League asks for prayer too.

4 HIM

(Marty Magehee, Kirk Sullivan, Andy Chrisman, Mark Harris)

Mark: The American Bible Society is close to 200 years

old. It's an organization whose primary function is to get the Word of God into each and every person's hand who lives on the face of this earth. I can't think of a more noble cause or a more worthwhile function. We've been involved with the American Bible Society for years, and it's been just an incredible relationship. We've been able to take a trip with them to Moscow and to stand on the street corners and pass out Bibles and to go into the hospitals where the little kids are and put into the hands of a little girl who's 8 or 9 years old. So it's been a rewarding experience for us because each and every night it takes the 4 HIM concert and makes it less of a local event and more of a global event. Each night we do a concert we give the people an opportunity to give to ABS and to help sponsor Bible distribution around the world. So that local concert really becomes a bigger event because it gives people the chance to become missionaries in some sort of way.

Andy: When you're out there handing the Bible out to people, you can't help but talk about it in the concerts because you see the power that rests within each one. You see what could happen if people let go of four bucks. Collectively over the course of the tour, you see those people in Moscow and hear the stories of those people in Siberia that go through four or five different forms of transportation just to get the Word out. It's a great way to be a missionary without having to leave your home in America.

Bryan Duncan

I've been impressed with ministries that are connected in some way to helping the world. I was impressed in the early days with James Dobson and **Focus on the Family.** I liked the fact that whether you were a Christian or not you understood the importance of relationships—understanding how to get along with your kids, how to raise them, understanding how to get along with your wife, your parents. I just noticed that people would listen to that and they were probably more open to the gospel because they knew that you were offering something that they recognized immediately as a need. With **Feed the Children,** it's the same kind of thing. People can recognize the need, and they can see that you are showing your love for God by doing something that anyone can identify as a good thing. I think people are drawn to Christ easier that way than by any other means. I understand the preaching of the Word is the ultimate thing, but they know you're Christians by your love. I think the best way to show that is by doing things that people recognize.

Our many blessings make us aware of the need to help others who are less fortunate than ourselves. Here Crystal Lewis talks about teaching the next generation.

Crystal Lewis

When I look into my kids' eyes and see that they're well fed, they're healthy, and they're happy, it gives me a whole new outlook on life to know that there are kids who aren't. They're not healthy, and they're not happy. They're not well fed. So it's exciting to have an opportunity to educate my kids, as young as they are, on helping others.

Bob Carlisle

I have seen poverty before in my lifetime, but for me to experience it not only through my eyes, but through the eyes of my children made a big difference for me. The great contrast between societies in the Dominican Republic is remarkable. There are some areas in the

Dominican Republic that are as posh as any resort community that exists on this planet. Yet, it is very closely guarded to within just city blocks to the kind of medieval poverty I didn't think even existed anymore. People washing their clothes, going to the bathroom, and drinking all in the same water.

Toilets that are basically just holes in the ground that eventually bleed into their water systems. This is all literally blocks away from one of the finest, upscale beach resorts I've ever seen.

My children understand and I want them to know: To whom much is given, much is required. I don't want my children to see their dad, having been given a platform—especially the platform that I've been given on a family issue [the song "Butterfly Kisses"] and not be able to use it somehow to give back. Because what I've sung about is so family-oriented, I thought it would be a perfect evolution to involve my children and my family in the work of **Food for the Hungry.** To be more than just a guy who stands up as a figurehead and says, "Look at the pictures of the starving children; come on, give some money." We see that a lot. We've become numb to it. I wanted these folks to see that my children and my wife and I are involved in this process.

You just want to come in and almost look on a society as Jesus would look on a society, saying, "How can I serve this? What can I do to love on these people and to make the existence that they have even better?"

As much as money is, time is also a precious contribution to give to the work of ministry. Early on, before Andy Hawthorne of The World Wide Message Tribe was in a band, he found himself pulling away more and more from his business and giving his energies to teenagers in Manchester, England.

World Wide Message Tribe
(Andy Hawthorne)

Well, I've always lived in Manchester. I was born and bred here. I moved down to Wales for a few months, but apart from that I've lived my whole life in Manchester. When I left school, I went into the fashion business. For quite a few years we had a fashion business in the heart of Manchester until I went full-time into ministry. That's what we consider this. We're not just musicians, but we definitely consider ourselves evangelists and ministers, going into the schools all over Manchester to talk about the incredible Good News about Jesus.

Now, in the fashion business, we were making "wacky hats" and some clothing and embroidery. We were mainly selling accessories to the big chain stores. And even that in all the time I was running this business, I was pulling out as much as I possibly could to do evangelism, because evangelism has always been my heart. I wanted to see young people in Manchester presented with the gospel in a way that makes sense to them. So I had my brother there, who's a Christian. In fact, I became a Christian through him, so he was totally into this as well.

I was putting on events at the big theaters in Manchester; I was the evangelist at the end of the evening and my mate, Mark Pennells, was in one of the bands who were playing. After he'd played at one of these events where about 20,000 young people came over a week and we saw hundreds and hundreds become Christians, Mark came to see me and my brother. He was trying to be a pop star, and at that time he was getting secular success. He came to see me and my brother and said, "I want to forget all that, forget trying to be successful and famous. All I want to do is evangelism like you guys. Will you help me go into schools?" When we saw his heart we prayed with him and talked it through. We knew this was something that we wanted to support. So a few of the guys chipped in some money to get Mark on the road initially just on his own, going around to schools, talking about his faith, doing his concerts on Friday, and I would do the evangelism. We also had a friend who had a little studio in his house and we started playing around together. So, originally, it was just me and Mark going into schools.

I was pulling out of the business as much as I could. The two of us started doing this music together and we got such an amazing buzz from the kids that we actually formed this band. And the band grew, so there are now eleven members in the World Wide Message Tribe, plus there are about fifty volunteers who work every week with us going into schools all over Manchester and occasionally doing big festivals and media stuff. But our real heart and our focus are still those schools, even with all the buzz that's going for the World Wide Message Tribe. There's something like a million teenagers in our patch in greater Manchester. It's one of the most densely populated populations of young people in Europe. And we feel that that is our thing—to try and present the age-old gospel message, be faithful to the truth of it, but present it in a way that makes sense to them. So that's what **Message to Schools** and the Tribe are all about.

Charity is our opportunity to get in line with the work of God. Incredible things happen when we are listening for God, living for Him, and seeking His direction. When we come in contact with His spirit the outcome is nothing less than extraordinary.

8 EXTRAORDINARY STORIES

> **"We do not remember days, we remember moments."**
>
> **Cesare Pavese**

THERE HAVE BEEN HUNDREDS. And hundreds and hundreds. But if I were to write out all of the stories I've heard now from artists, this book would be the size of an old King James Bible with concordance.

Artists are blessed with interesting lives. They travel constantly. They've crisscrossed this country so many times that the last thing they want to do is use all the frequent flyer miles they've chalked up. And they've met gobs of people. So I began asking them about the people they meet and the things that they see. Primarily, I was interested in what kind of feedback the artists were getting from the people who attend their concerts and buy their music. It wasn't meant as a pop quiz (no pun intended) or a measurement of an artist's ministry by any means. I simply wanted to know if this music, this genre, these songs, this running all around the country was having any impact on *real people*.

Well, they did have stories.

Hundreds.

That line of questioning has richly expanded ever since. Not only do I now ask how an artist's ministry has touched someone else, I ask how they themselves are changed, because I've heard the stories of a once anonymous record-buying public to whom these artists started out ministering over the distance of radio airwaves and through recorded work.

So we began collecting the stories from artists on their encounters with numerous people who briefly entered their lives but changed them permanently.

That's what this chapter is all about: the stories of encounters with people and events that have changed forever the teller of the tale. Like Margaret Becker in this first story, perhaps we will be forever changed as well.

Margaret Becker

Something that happened this past fall tour was really a life-changing moment for me. It was that point that I think we all come to from time to time, when we're going one way and we abruptly go the other way because of an interaction or an event.

My event was a young boy named Juan. I had received a letter through the mail at my management company that this boy wanted to talk with me after the show. I thought, *His mom went through a lot of trouble to write the letter, so I'm definitely going to go.*

Basically the letter just said that he was ill and wanted to see me.

Well, I waited before the show to meet them, and they never came. I waited during a different segment of time, and they didn't come. Then finally at the very last minute as I was walking out of the building someone stopped me and said, "Juan and his mom are here." So I turned around and there was an extraordinary five-year-old boy who was completely dressed in a three-piece suit. He offered his hand to me. He spoke to me like an adult—you know, "Hello, Margaret" and shook my hand. And he had a camera, "Okay, Mom, take our picture" and orchestrated the whole thing. He himself wanted to take his own picture of me. He handed me this bear that he had bought for me along with a note that basically he just dictated and then signed his name.

I was really just moved at how mature he was and how incredibly well organized he was. I was very curious about what his illness was and what would become of him. I took everything he gave me back to my room and immediately opened it up when I got there. I read first the letter from his mom that said Juan had a brain tumor. In all the time he had gone through scans and also chemotherapy and radiation therapy, he had never once had a sedative or a pain killer. The hospital was astounded because he was the only child that they knew of who never took any medication while undergoing treatment. All he would do is take my last album *Soul* and listen to it while he was receiving his therapy. He didn't ever complain—nothing at all like that. Apparently, the woman wrote that the last time she took him in the doctor told her, "Enjoy him, because he won't be coming back." It was his last session, and she said he only had a few weeks.

During those two or three weeks, he came to see me. One of the final things he wanted to do was to meet me. I don't know that I have the vocabulary or the artistic integrity to express what that felt like. To know that somebody's last wish was *to meet me.* Someone as insignificant and dismissable as myself. How humbling and then how moving to think that this young life was going to end soon. All that in light of me wishing that I could roll the tape back and go back to that moment and make it more of a moment—wishing I could have taken him somewhere, that I could have taken him for coffee or done something more, although he didn't request it and he wasn't anxious for it. Yet, it made me stop and assess. I need to pay more attention to these things. I need to be more informed, and

I need to realize that these are the moments that count. These are the things that we walk away with. It's not anything else. It's not how many people came to the show or how well you sang or didn't sing. It's the interaction with people.

We feel for everyone in Margaret's story: We feel the pain of the young boy's illness, the mother's approaching loss of her child, and the narrator's deep regret. But are we able to learn the lessons that others teach us?

Joshua 1:9 states, "Have I not commanded you? Be strong and courageous. Do not be terrified; do not be discouraged, for the Lord your God will be with you wherever you go." Steve Camp provides us with a living example of this verse in the story below.

Steve Camp

Many years ago I was touring in Canada, doing a series of concerts at various churches and schools, but there was one very unusual and special evening—a stand-out event that I have never forgotten. In Eastern Canada there is a group of people known as Satan's Choice—the Canadian complement to the Hell's Angels here in the U.S. I was informed that this group had been allowed to hold meetings at a certain university near the St. Catherine area, but Christians were not being allowed to hold concerts, prayer meetings, or Bible studies in the same facility. Through much prayer I was given permission to do the first Christian music concert there at this school. It was thrilling!

During the day of the concert, while lights and sound were being hoisted up in place, some of these local Satanists were calling the stagehands backstage and saying, "If this Christian singer, Steve Camp, sings about

Jesus tonight we're going to kill him." This was obviously disturbing news to me. I arrived at the concert about an hour ahead of time, as I usually do, to meet and pray with the counselors and get ready for the evening's events. Just then someone approached me, informing me that the head of the Satanic coven was on the phone and wondered if I wanted to take his call. Seeing that I don't get too many phone calls from Satanists (in fact this was the first and only one I have ever had), I said that I would definitely talk with him as long as he was not calling collect.

The man on the other end of the phone told me that there were fifty members in his coven and said to me, "If you sing about Jesus tonight and preach the Gospel we're going to hurt you." I told him the truth of what the Apostle Paul said in Philippians 1:21 when he proclaimed, "For me to live is Christ and to die is gain" (and advised him to take his best shot). He said, "You mean you're not afraid of our god?" I answered him by asserting as boldly as I could, "What god? Satan is not God! He's a created being, a fallen angel, walking around with a crushed head—doesn't sound like much of a god to me." I told him that if they weren't doing anything tonight besides plotting my death, I'd like to invite them out to be my guests at the concert that evening. He asked me, "How will we get in?" A bit surprised, I told him that I would leave fifty complimentary tickets at the back of the auditorium for the visiting Satanists in that community.

According to the ticket count, we had 45 Satanists attend the concert that night—and it was awesome! All through the invitation while sharing the Gospel, these men and women were trying to be disruptive—throwing things at me on the stage and ministering to me in an interesting form of Greek language. I told them I would talk to them afterwards and asked several times politely for them to please sit down and be quiet. They did not. Finally, I forcefully said, "In the name of Jesus Christ, *sit down.*" And they *all* sat down! (My motto to this day is "Walk softly and carry a big Bible!")

At the end of the invitation that evening, and I say this only in praise of our Lord and as a spectator of God's grace, thirty out of those forty-five Satanists received Jesus Christ as their Lord and Savior. To God be the glory, great things He has done!

Spiritual battle is real. We wrestle not against flesh and blood, do we, beloved? The Lord used yet another circumstance to glorify Himself, to reveal to me the inadequacy of my own strength, and to further galvanize my life with the reality that Satan may be mighty but our Lord Jesus Christ is *Almighty.* We never have to fear the enemy of our soul for he has been conquered by the Captain of Salvation forever. We need to remember that "greater is He who is in us than he who is in the world."

How do we have victory in the daily warfare of living for Christ? By putting on the full armor of God—that is, obedient holy living. Submit to God, resist the devil and he will flee from you. That is a promise, beloved—not a magic formula or some spiritual incantation, but real Christianity put into practice everyday. To *submit* means to live under the authority of another. Live this very moment, Christian, under the authority of God's Word in obedience to Christ empowered by the Holy Spirit. And it's that character of life lived in holiness before the Lord that is sufficient to stand against the wiles of the devil . . . and he will flee.

By the way, next time you do an outreach in your community, invite the local occult groups and Satanists to attend the meeting. It tends to put a little edge on the night, but what a tremendous opportunity for evangelism. RUN TO THE BATTLE!

A song's worshipful message recorded in Nashville is heard all over the country. Uplifting statements made in a national magazine are read from coast to coast. Without meeting one another, we are admonished by the messages of meaning coming from the lips of other believers. The following example should teach us that people whom we've never seen may be in need of just the kind of message we singularly possess.

Lisa Bevill

When I was recording the song "All Because of You" I just kept thinking about the young girls who had been writing to me in response to an article I did for *Brio* magazine. There was a three-page article within the magazine that talked about my life and my struggles as a teenager growing up with chronically ill parents. I had such an incredible response from those girls writing in. Their letters just absolutely wiped me out. I sat every night on my couch just poring over their letters and weeping.

I wept because there are so many young girls who are hurting out there about the way they look. They hate themselves. They can't talk to their parents and they don't have any friends. They're so wrapped up in how they look and who they are. They can't find God and they can't find peace in their lives even though most of them are Christian girls! They read the article, and it touched them. I received letters saying things like, "I didn't know anyone else felt like I did" and "If you could make it so can I."

I tried to write all the girls back. At first, I wrote just a very personalized letter to all of them that addressed specifically their issues. All of the girls who were writing in were all saying the same things! They were all asking the same questions. At the end of that letter I asked them to go to their mirror. I said, "I want you to look in the mirror, and

I want you to tell yourself that you love yourself, no matter what you look like. No matter what you see, I want you to see something beautiful and not something ugly. I want you to love what God created, and I hope you will find the beauty in the mirror when you look there again." I had to do that when I was a young teenager. Someone in counseling encouraged me to do that because I was just so wrapped up in acceptance of what I looked like and what I did.

I wanted to record a song that was really special for the girls. I wanted the girls to know that it was for them, so that they would know that I had read each of their letters. Only the girls who read what I wrote on the song dedication will know who this song is for. I wrote, "I pray that you looked in the mirror and found the beauty." I wanted those girls to feel really special. I wanted them to feel like I was reaching out to them. I wanted that song to minister to them.

It's not just the story that moves us, it's the passion in which it is told. Lisa Bevill's empathy for the girls came from her own well of experiences as a teenager, while in this next story, Crystal Lewis finds she is the recipient of a gift more momentous than the one she's readying herself to give.

Crystal Lewis

I sang at a church in California one night. After the concert, this little girl came up to me with her mom. She was around seven or eight years old, and she was blind. Her mom told me that she listened to my music all the time and then she asked, well, the little girl was wondering if she could touch my face! And I just couldn't control my reaction. I was crying. I mean just try to even imagine, what those of us with two seeing eyes can't imagine: being blind. I was just instantly struck by what a blessing it is just to be able to see.

Words can't even describe what it felt like to let this little girl feel my face. I tried to imagine what was going on in her mind. It was really an intense moment for me. There were a zillion other people standing all around us. I tried to put everything else out of my mind and say, "Wow, God, this is a special person. This is a special moment."

In *Jurassic Park,* scientists bring dinosaurs into contemporary times through genetic engineering. Listening to English-born Andy Hawthorne of The World Wide Message Tribe, one gets the sense we are hearing a character "transported" through time to us from the Book of Acts. In this narrative, his faith is tested by a young girl who is asking not only if Jesus is real, she's asking for proof.

World Wide Message Tribe

(Andy Hawthorne)

I met a girl two weeks ago at a church whom I well remember coming to see me at the end of a service we did two and a half years ago in a church in a place called Marple. She came to see me at the end of that service. Her name was Sabrina, and she had that "*Life's given me a bad deal*" look on her face. She was obviously just having a terrible time. She was having the most appalling fits, every two days she'd been taken out of normal school. She just came to me and said, "I want to be a Christian, but how can it be fair that Jesus lets me have these fits?" I explained to her that *it wasn't Jesus who gave her the fits.* She said, "I want you to pray that Jesus will take them away." Well, you know, it's kind of a scary thing, but I put my hand on that girl after we prayed and sorted out that she really meant business. She became a Christian, and I put my hand on her and prayed for her with all the faith I could muster. I asked Jesus to sort out this problem.

I didn't see her again because she went off to some other church and we were traveling around Manchester. Then two weeks ago, she came to see me and she said, "Do you remember me?"

I did remember and I said, "*Sabrina?*" She looked different, so I asked her how she'd been going on. She said she'd never had another fit since that day two and a half years ago. It's exciting that Jesus wanted to heal her, but what's far more exciting is that she's a Christian going on with God. It's all right being healed of a physical ailment, but what's far more exciting is having your sins forgiven, being set free, and being given a place in heaven for all eternity.

If we believe God's miracles of physical healing belong in another century—story after countless story will prove us to be mistaken. Here's yet another testimony of God's power to heal us.

4 HIM

(Marty Magehee, Kirk Sullivan, Andy Chrisman, Mark Harris)

Marty: Back in September of 1994, I contracted a rare form of arthritis that crippled me from the waist down. It afflicted every joint from below my waist including the little bones in my feet, my right collarbone, my right wrist, and my right thumb. For about seven months the pain was excruciating. There were a lot of nights where darkness was not merely a state of absence of light: It was something much deeper.

I remember the guys in 4 HIM had to go through this affliction with me because of our schedule. They would help me on stage and off each night. They would help me get from point A to point B. My wife had to help me through everything not only at home, but also on the road. She took care of my luggage and got me around. That's humbling, having your wife take care of you.

On March 14, 1995, God completely healed me, and I haven't had any occurrence of the arthritis ever since. It was during that time of illness that I really held on to Psalm 91, where God promises us a divine protection to preserve us through whatever it is that the enemy has in store for us. Like when Satan went to God and said that his servant Job would curse Him if given a chance in a time of testing. God knew Job's heart and allowed Satan to do whatever he wanted, short of killing him, because God knew that Job would never turn his back on Him.

We still are tested today. It was a testing that I am honored to have gone through, although I didn't see it that way at the time. Now I'm able to step back and look at it. God trusted me enough to allow me to walk through this thing and to come out the other side still serving Him.

All of the people in Marty's story give us an example of love in action. They each had no idea how long his illness would go on. Yet instead of replacing him, they helped him on and off stage each night, carrying his luggage and getting him around. Today they remain intact as one of the most celebrated and creative groups in contemporary Christian music.

From the four corners of the world, people are hearing and responding to God's Spirit woven into the fabric of contemporary Christian music. In times of great sorrow, in our moments of weakness, and when we need conviction most, music ministers to us, bringing solace and renewal.

Michael Card

It's hard to come up with just one story about the people I've heard from who've heard my music. There are pictures up on my mantelpiece of babies whose parents have cut off their life support and listened to "Sleep Sound in Jesus" holding their babies while they died.

I think the story that I remember most is from years ago. A man wrote me a letter and said he'd been having an affair with this woman. He was going to leave his wife and three little girls. There was a woman at the hotel waiting for him. He was just leaving a note behind and then slipping away in his car, too much a coward to confront his family. In the car on the way to the hotel to pick up this woman that he was going to leave town with, he heard the song "Love Crucified Arose" playing. And the Lord used that song to convict him. He pulled off the road and sat there and wept, and I guess he got real with the Lord. He turned around, went home, called the motel, and told the woman that he wouldn't be coming. He confessed everything to his wife. Months after getting his letter, the family came to one of my concerts and I got to meet them. Here was this beautiful woman and three beautiful little girls. He was willing at one time to throw them all away.

Having told that story, two others come to mind about a couple of missionaries. Max Lucado was one of them. When Max was still a missionary in South America, he at one point was going to quit. He was going to give up his calling, but someone gave him a tape. I think it was "Love Crucified Arose" there, too. He heard that song and realized again the calling God placed on his life. We started exchanging letters before he had even written any books. I knew Max as a missionary before I knew him as an author.

I've had a couple of different missionary stories like that where people were going to give up. There was a

Chinese missionary, a guy who was on a bus. It was one of those horrible old buses with hard wooden seats that you ride for days just to get anywhere in China. This missionary had left where God had called him to be, sort of like Jonah, I guess. Anyway, he had gotten ahold of my record *Poiema,* and on his long bus ride, when he didn't have anything else to do, he listened to it over and over again. Finally, he turned around and made the twenty-hour trip back the other way. He decided that staying in China was what God called him to do.

Those are the stories I sometimes hear. And again, it might have been any song. God can use the rocks to praise Him if He wants to. He gives us the privilege of having a part in and doing our thing in fulfillment of His purpose. That's the real privilege when you do hear stories like that. I've had people from, you know . . . Borneo and just the edge of the earth write and tell me those kinds of things. How does a tape even get out there to begin with?

Patsy Cline, Buddy Holly, and Stevie Ray Vaughn. The history of modern music is filled with tragic accounts of recording artists killed in plane crashes. Whether it's because Al Denson's story puts us in the cockpit with those other artists or because in his version death is cheated, his tale is both riveting and powerful. Some experiences are just too frightening not to impact us.

Al Denson

One afternoon I was headed into San Antonio, Texas, aboard a small plane with a couple of pilots. We were coming in for a landing when the engine in the airplane just shut off. All of a sudden we knew for about forty-five seconds afterward that we were going to crash. We did all the things that we could, but there was no way to get out of it.

A lot of things went through my mind in those forty-five seconds. I wondered if I'd ever see my wife again or my friends or my family. I thought about what would be the outcome of the crash and all the while we were barreling toward the ground. It's hard to have peace at a time like that, but I did have peace because of what Christ did on the cross. Because of that I knew I would see my family and friends again, because all of us are Christians.

It's really kind of an eye-opener, to say the least. We hit the ground, they cut us out of the airplane, and about three days later I woke up in the hospital. It was then that I found out one of my best friends, the pilot, had died just an hour before. The other passenger was fine.

Recovery was especially difficult. I remember asking my wife if I had any arms or legs, because I didn't know. I couldn't feel them. I didn't know what had happened to me, either. I asked her if I was okay because I couldn't see. I knew she was there only because of her voice. She told me I had 500 stitches in my face and both my legs and arms were broken. They would later give me a new nose.

I kept thinking how lucky I was to be alive with all that was wrong with me. I was glad the Lord gave me another chance to live. I could still remember thinking just before I hit, *God, am I going to live?* The only thing I had to turn to was my relationship with Christ. It boils down to this: If someone tells you that you've got just forty-five seconds to live, what are you going to do? Who are you going to want to see?

From there it was a series of steps in my rehabilitation: bones, stitches, and plastic surgeons. My record company, Benson, was really cool. My record was scheduled to begin recording two days before the crash. Their response was so caring and loving. They came down and set up a recording studio in my house. It gave me something to do other than just sit there and relive the nightmare over and over again. They moved out the furniture, set up the equipment, and I recorded my vocals right there in my home. I'd get out of bed. They'd set me on a stool, I'd sing until I was tired, and they'd throw me back in bed. That's how the whole album [*Do You Know This Man?*] was recorded. In fact, I had to give one of my producers, Paul Mills, a new set of headphones because I had bled all over his during those recordings.

Most of my recovery time was spent trying to answer that one three-letter word: *Why?*

My first thought was just gratitude. Gratitude that God gave me a chance to live because I thought I was not going to make it. Then I went from that to working through my friend passing away and dealing with watching my wife having to help me do everything. Seeing her suffer made me start to get angry at God. I wondered "Why did You do this to me? I was out 200 days on the road last year for You! This is not fair!" One day I was lying in bed crying, and my dad came in to see me. I told him I just couldn't believe this had happened. I said, "Dad, when I see Jesus, I'm going to have a lot of questions." My dad just sat there until I wasn't sure if he was going to answer at all. Finally, he said, "Son, when you see Him, it's not going to matter."

He's right. I began to think about other people who had lost their loved ones to cancer, automobile accidents, and other things. We don't understand it always, but thank God there's hope.

Al Denson lived to tell a story that, thankfully, few of us will experience. His story punctuates the urgency to share the gospel with those around us. In 1995, Kenny Marks's family experienced God's reconciliation and healing for an event thought long in the past.

Kenny Marks

My wife, Pamela, and I have been married a long time. Back when we had just first met each other she told me something about herself I'd never been told before. She said "Kenny, I just want to tell you something up front, right at the beginning of this relationship, about something that happened when I was younger. When I was 16 and growing up in West Virginia, one of the hardest things happened to me." I said, "What are you talking about?" because I really didn't know. She said, "Well, I had a relationship with a boy. It was a sad time in my life, but I became pregnant, and the best thing that my parents and I thought we could do was to have the baby and to put it up for adoption." And that's what she did. She had the baby, and the baby was put up for adoption March 4, a long time ago.

Well, our relationship grew, and about two years after she told me that story, we were married. On March 4 of last year our telephone rang here in Nashville, and the voice on the other end of the phone said, "Is this Pamela Marks?" and my wife said, "Yes?" She said, "Well, my name's Christy. I just wanted to ask you, if today, March 4, means anything to you?" And my wife was really shocked. It was amazing, but she had the mind to say, "You know what, this day really does mean a lot to me, and I'd love to meet you and tell you about it."

That was Christy on the other end of the line, this daughter who had now grown up. She was adopted by a lovely, Christian family in West Virginia. She always knew she was adopted. She would go with her mom to the grocery store as a little girl and pull on her mother's skirt and ask, "Is that my mommy over there?" and her adopted mother would say, "No, honey, that's not her, but maybe someday you'll meet her." And sure enough, about a week after getting that phone call, Pam got on a plane here in Nashville, and Christy got on a plane in her city, and they both flew to this little town in West Virginia, where they met for the first time.

I wanted to write about that event because of the importance of the whole idea of reconciliation in our relationships. We're born into this world *with a God that cares about us,* no matter what kind of difficulty we might be born into. Certainly, being born and immediately adopted at birth would be a tough one. But God is good and He wants us to reconcile our lives to one another and to Him.

The story of Pam and Christy needed to be told. So I wrote the song "In My Mother's Eyes" to tell a little bit about the hope and the dream and the wish in the mind's eye of the adopted child to one day meet that person who really brought them into this world. I wrote that song to tell that story for Pam and for Christy.

Mothers pray for daughters (even if they haven't yet learned their names). At first, you may think Tammy Trent's story is about God's protection over us (and it is), but moreover, it's about a mother's love and the power of prayer.

Tammy Trent

I was invited to perform for Youth with a Mission during the 1996 Summer Olympics in Atlanta. I went on stage about 11:00 P.M. and finished up around midnight. I had brought a band with me, and they wanted to go downtown and see James Brown. So my husband, Trent, and I gave them some money and just said, "Go and have a great time." We were just going to walk around, so we went over to the Centennial Park. We walked right through the Swatch building, came out, and stood by a place called "The Tower."

We stood there about five minutes watching the band "Jack Mack and the Heart Attack." I was so comfortable there and actually was really enjoying the music. Trent asked if I wanted to walk away and see some other stuff, and I said, "No, I really want to just sit here. Can you give me a couple more minutes?" So he did. A few minutes after that he said, "Come on, let's go!" I remember him pulling me away, and I left my spot unwillingly and went along with him.

Two minutes after we walked away from that spot, the Olympic park bomb *hidden in the tower just feet from where we had been standing exploded.* Both of us were immediately thrown to the ground. I can remember instantly standing back up and just freaking out! People were running and screaming and crying. I started crying, too, not knowing what was going on. When Trent spoke to me I couldn't hear him very well. I had ruptured an eardrum as a result of being so close to the explosion.

I felt a rush of emotion from realizing how blessed and fortunate I was to be alive. We heard about the loss of life there and saw firsthand the injuries. We were standing *so close* to the tower. If we had not left when we did, I believe we could have been seriously injured, and who knows if we would be alive today. Even the Swatch building that we had walked through was partly destroyed by the bomb blast.

I believe very strongly that the Holy Spirit was telling Trent to get us out of there. Stubbornly, I wanted to stay, but I'm thankful that Trent listened to the Holy Spirit and that he listens for the Word of God. It's hard to imagine that we could have died, but it's definitely a reality.

That event brought back to me the reality of people praying for me. My mom especially covers me in prayer every day. Sometimes before I would call home and tell *mom* what was going on and she'd say, "Okay, honey, can I pray for you?" And if I'm in the middle of the airport with only minutes to catch a plane, I want to say, "Okay, but hurry." I don't do that anymore. I tell her, "Mom, you can pray all day." So this brought back to me the reality of the power of prayer. There's importance in people praying for a ministry. Angels are always looking out for us. God had a plan for me, and it wasn't my time to go. Jesus has got something planned, I don't know what it is, but I'm ready. It's obvious the devil wants to stop those things, but I'm alive.

Talented singers have no monopoly on changing lives. Humility and servanthood, exhibited by anyone, can be the beginning of reaching out to others. Over a lifetime, we all have opportunities to show genuine caregiving to the people who need us. That penetrating reality begs us to consider this profound question: Over a lifetime, how many others does a faithful servant of Jesus Christ touch?

Andrae Crouch

Since I've been a pastor here in California, and everyone seems to know how to find me, I've heard from people all over the world. It's been a blessing. Of course, I hear from those who have been touched from this song or that song. It seems like there has been just an overabundance of responses.

I heard from a guy who left a message on my answering machine. He said, "I hope this is Andrae Crouch's number. I just wanted to let you know that twenty years ago I heard the gospel of Jesus Christ at your concert.

Today I am the pastor of a 2,000-member church in Toronto, Canada, and I just wanted to thank you."

Recently, I just happened to sit in one of Carman's concerts. I had known that he had been influenced by my music and he had gotten saved through my music. He had called me up and said, "Andrae, will you please come to one of my concerts?" He gave me his cellular phone number and said he would be in southern California and he asked me to call him. He said, "You've never seen what your ministry has done. I want you to see the fruit of your labor. Please come and see me." So I was blessed to go see him, and I felt like a father looking at his son. It was a joy to see all the kids who were coming and all the kids who got saved. I was so proud of him.

It's been such a blessing when people come into the church. Some with testimonies. Some of them I don't even recognize because they were so young when they were saved at one of our meetings. We get reports of healing. Even yesterday, a gentleman was telling me that he was left to die, but a song had given him hope during that time, and now he's alive and going to preach. I've just heard from people all over the world. I'll be going to Fiji soon by the request of some of the people who got saved years ago through our ministry. It just blows me away.

If a person will really give his or her talent and life to the Lord, and let God bless it and multiply it, they will see results for their labors. We won't see all of it this side of heaven, but God sends testimonies through people just when we need them most.

Angie and Debbie Winans give us some insights on growing up in a house of faith. Their story shows that we can hear about God's provisions over and over, but nothing clues us in quite like a good old-fashioned demonstration.

Angie & Debbie Winans

Debbie: My mom had a lot of kids, and my dad always had a lot of energy for Jesus. When you have a lot of kids, sometimes food is thin. I used to ask, "Why do I have to wait to eat tomorrow? Why can't I just eat?" *"No, no, no, the Lord's going to provide."* That's all we ever heard, *"The Lord's going to provide."* I was saying, "Look, what kind of Lord are you all serving? Because I'm hungry and He ain't providing."

But during those times when I thought it was the bottom, I only saw my dad and my mom worship God like we were living on the tiptop, filthy-rich in a large home; but we weren't. I looked at them and I thought, *They're crazy! They are brainwashed!* But what they learned, or should I say what I learned, is that's what God loves most: that you worship Him in spite of everything. Then He brings you into an open field where there's milk flowing. You have blessings that you don't have room to receive when you learn the lesson that you worship God just to worship Him for Him being God, no matter what He does or doesn't give you. Because He has it all. He wants to know if you love Him for Him. That's what we were taught. My father instilled in us, "You love God, you love each other—*everything else will work itself out.*"

So Jesus was in my mind all the time, but I wanted to be like the other kids at school. I wanted to dance and I wanted to cuss. I couldn't understand why I couldn't cuss. I couldn't do anything. I thought, *This church stuff is just driving me crazy!*

My mom always taught us, "If you ever get in trouble, call on Jesus." I used to think, *Yeah, yeah, all right,* until I was walking home from school one day, and this man mugged me. He jumped out in front of me, and I looked at him like, *This is not happening.* We lived off of a busy street, but every car had stopped; there was nothing. He went to grab at a necklace I had on and grabbed so hard that he knocked me to the ground. Then he straddled on top of me with his legs and bent down. I thought, *Oh my God, I'm about to be raped and killed, and there's no one around!*

I was looking around. Where'd all the cars go? Under my breath I kept saying, "Jesus, Jesus, Jesus . . ." He said, "*What'd you say?*" and I said, "Jesus?" He said, "*Don't say that!*" I said, "Oh, Jesus," because I saw this thing worked. I started saying, "The blood of Jesus," remembering my mother saying, "*Call on the blood of Jesus.*" So I said, "The blood of Jesus!" and the man got up and ran! He was *so mad* at me for calling that name, but he ran.

After that, I went into my house because it had really disturbed me. I thought, *This is deep.* I was looking for cars, but they weren't coming. I have seven brothers, but no one was home. They all could have beat him up, but they weren't there. So I realized, *Jesus did it. I called His name and the man ran.* The spirit that was leading that man said, "Don't call *that* name!" When I realized that name was powerful, I said, "I've got to know who He is."

Ever since that day, I stopped going to church because I *had* to. I started going because I wanted to know who in the world He was. Who is Jesus that people could get scared just by hearing His name? I went to the back of the Bible to find out who in the world is Jesus. I looked up the word "*Jesus*" in the concordance. I got all the things that He did, and then I read the stories about Him. I've just been fascinated with Him ever since because His name is powerful.

Angie: My father put the blood of Jesus in us heavy. We went for the longest time without a lock on our door, but nobody ever broke into our house [in Detroit, Michigan]. Because in the wee hours of the night we would be awakened by my father praying, *"the blood of Jesus, the blood of Jesus . . ."* Coming in to our room, he put a blessing on us, *"the blood of Jesus, the blood of Jesus . . ."* We watched him live the life and he put it in us. Then he would put little things in us like, "When people say you sang well, get that glory off of you. That's not your glory. Say, 'Praise God.'" So people laugh at us today because we'll say "Praise God" in a minute. But my dad put that in us when we were children.

Spiritual things taught to Angie and Debbie as children still surface in their interviews today. Every one of the ten-member Winans family has been influenced by the faith of their parents, Delores and David "Skip" Winans. Today nine of the Winans children are involved with musical ministries, a list that includes BeBe and CeCe Winans.

9 LIFE'S RUGGED CROSSES

"We are all angels with one wing, and we need each other to fly."

John Hagee

TWENTY YEARS AGO, Steven Spielberg directed *Close Encounters of the Third Kind*, a movie about aliens visiting our planet. The ad that went out with that movie claimed, "We Are Not Alone." Whether or not there are aliens somewhere out there who want to come over for a visit, I don't know. But in many ways more germane to us here on earth, we are in fact feeling very much alone.

The rain falls on us all. Difficulties come into every life, and we face struggles of all sorts that bend us to the point of breaking. We've all been there, or we are there, or we're on our way there. Are you going through the toughest season of your life now at this moment? Let me share with you a surprising miracle. When we hear of others' difficulties, it makes us feel not so alone. When we share our own struggles with others, finding their acceptance, love, and prayers, God is present and love abounds. God connects us *together* in such a way that His love and His people restore us.

Oddly enough, I find traces of this happening in contemporary Christian music. We have the *sharing* and the *listening* going on by artists who candidly present their deepest selves through their music and interviews.

This chapter is about sharing the tough times, surviving them, and turning them into good.

We don't know when our troubles will appear. We don't know when they will depart. Whenever someone in one of these stories is in a challenging circumstance, he or she is usually alone. How sad. Our struggles should be shared. When the light comes breaking through their darkness, it is always carried by another or Christ. Our happiness and healing are found in connection with God and with others. Together, "We Can Make a Difference" sings Jaci Velasquez. Maybe Spielberg was right after all.

This interview with Bonnie Keen of First Call was an extension of the very first interview that we ever conducted on *Soul2Soul*. Early in the spring of 1994, Bonnie had graciously agreed to be the initial guest on an untried radio program called *Soul2Soul*. Although the program wouldn't air for another five months, we asked her to help us produce a "pilot" to demonstrate what we were trying to do.

Scandal broke out just shortly after the Dove Awards in April, involving an affair between the newest member of First Call, Mary Beth Jordan, and Gospel singer Michael English. Between the time of the media feeding frenzy served up by tabloid news and our debut in August of '94, we asked Bonnie to return to our studios and share the human story that was lost amidst the appetite for sensation.

First Call

(Marty McCall, Bonnie Keen)

Bonnie: The last eight weeks have been just about as difficult a time as I've gone through in my life—one of the lowest points for Marty and me, for Mary Beth and her family, and for Michael and his family. Paramount to everything, it has been the grieving and the tragedy of the lives that have been shattered by this. There are a lot of children involved who haven't been mentioned much. There's been a lot of talk about Dove Awards and records being pulled, and I think the real tragedy is not little pieces of metal and records; it's the people.

The first thing that went through my mind was Mary Beth's family, her husband, Michael's wife, Lisa, and his daughter, Megan, and people we just love and know are going to be forever changed by this situation. So on a personal level, because we're very good friends with Mary Beth, we have been grieving very much for her and her family. On a business level, which is a whole other side of it, this pretty much devastated First Call. It has been really difficult. Marty and I have looked at the last nine years of work and all of a sudden our names and faces are in the *National Enquirer* and tabloids and things that you never imagined happening. We spend a lot of time on our faces, saying to each other, "What does God want to happen now?" If First Call is resurrected out of this, we want it to be God's hand.

We really ask, "What does God want us to do now?" We don't want First Call necessarily to end this way. It's been staggering what it's done to us, personally and on a business level. It's been devastating, really devastating. We're praying a lot for restoration and healing in everybody's life. I don't know exactly how that's going to happen. That's definitely going to be an act of God, because coming back through this kind of thing is just a nightmare. It can be done, but it takes a lot of will on everybody's part. This situation—we had no idea what it was. We knew there was some danger Michael and Mary Beth were both walking in. It was addressed several times and prayerfully confronted with them. We were told that there wasn't a problem, and so we went on that assumption. So we were pretty shocked.

The preacher E. V. Hill once said, "The body of Christ is not made up of clean people, but of dirty people who are being washed clean by the blood of Jesus. It's not made up of well people, but of sick people, and some of us are getting better one day at a time. It's not made up of straight people, but of crooked people who are being straightened out by the Word of God" and I thought, *That's it—that's us.* We're all dirty and sick and crooked, and by the mercy of Jesus one day at a time we're all trying to get better.

Personally, it's made me look at the whole industry and question everything all over again and say, "*What are we doing—are we creating idols out of artists?*" There's a certain amount of idolatry that's gone on with it. There's a certain amount of hero worship.

It has been a dark, dark time. It has been depressing on many levels. The whole media thing has been totally crazy. It's been like a circus, and we've tried to stay out of it as much as possible. Marty and I feel we got lost in a lot of it, quite frankly. Every once in a while someone will say, "Oh, by the way is First Call still, ah, what are you doing?" like as an afterthought, and we feel this has just blown apart what we've worked on for the last decade. But God can do anything. God can restore and heal. So we're standing in that place right now with our families and in prayer for their families. We just ask anybody to do that, not to talk about it so much, but to pray about it a lot because that's where it's going to be fought now. That's where the battles are going to be fought.

If it were up to me we wouldn't have Dove Awards. There wouldn't be Dove Awards. The Grammys recognize Gospel artists—that's enough. Why do we have to create our own little series of events and idols and little statues? I think it feeds into a system that is not godly and a competitiveness that is not godly. I'm really kind of sick of that whole thing. I'm really ready to say let's just do away with that whole thing; it really doesn't serve any purpose. It really doesn't. I think there's so much emphasis put on the trappings of what we do that you can lose sight of what's really being done with it. What has happened is that God has allowed Christian music to continue because people respond to it from a pure place. Not because the artists are pure or because the industry is pure (it definitely isn't), but people respond to it. People are truly blessed by something that happens in the music. I think that's the only reason that God, in His mercy, has allowed it to continue.

The way Christian music started out was you had some artists like Keith Green who had a ministry that was going. Because of a fire in their hearts for God they were writing and singing about God. Then there became a market around that that took what he did or what the different artists did and tried to market it. We have now come to a place where we take somebody who looks good and sings well, and we try to create the heart, and it's backward. You know, you either have the heart for the ministry and you have the fire, or you don't. But we do it the way the world does it. We market our artists to be sexy. We market our artists to be this, that, and the other.

I think we really have to watch how we're caring for artists, where we put them, and where we place them. As an industry, we need to be very careful who the people are because it's a dangerous place to walk into where you have huge adulation by thousands and thousands of people.

Every time I get shaken in my life, it makes me even more defiant with the enemy to say I will not turn my back on what I believe. If I can only say that when I get out of bed somedays, "I still believe" and I'm going to hold on to that for the next 24 hours. Sometimes that's all I can do. This experience has been like that for me, but I'm determined to get on the other side of it.

They say there's nothing sadder than tears from a clown. Chonda Pierce is one of funniest women in American, but the story she shared with us told us something about the healing that goes on when we share.

Chonda Pierce

In growing up as a preacher's kid, I experienced some tragedy as many people do. My twenty-year-old sister was killed in a car accident very suddenly and it changed things for us. We all had great plans of what we wanted to do, but ours included each other: We were going to travel and sing as a group. You know, we wanted to be a Southern Gospel quartet . . . we had the polyester (that was a joke). We really had these plans, but when Sharlotta was killed, a lot of grief set in for our family like it does for many. My father became very discouraged, very depressed. Soon after my little sister became very ill. We found out she had leukemia. She was fifteen. Twenty-one days later she died a very slow and agonizing death. And it wasn't funny. My father in all of that left the ministry. My brother had married and moved away.

I will never forget the sights and the scenes that stick out in my head from my childhood. One in particular was the day my mother and I had a great big yard sale because we had to get out of the parsonage. A new pastor was coming and we had to sell our home, our part of it. We put just about everything that we owned in the yard. I went into the bathroom and painted on a clown face. I mean literally. I put a triangle nose on and white face and little rosy cheeks and red yarn hair and was Raggedy Andy all day long with a great big sign that said, "Everything's gotta go"—out in the street ushering cars into our yard.

I had learned firsthand what you can do when you put a mask on and you hide behind your laugh or your sarcasm or your bitterness. It was not funny. That kind of laugh and that kind of humor will just wear you out and you can't find peace. There is no medicine in it.

It was a long journey for me to actually remove the mask and to find what peace and comfort is really all about. When I put my trust in God and put my faith in Him, the bitterness kind of subsides, and the sarcasm begins to leave, and what is left is really good genuine laughter, even in the tough days. I learned that the hard way. My mom, in all of that, was one of those people who stood strong and faithful in front of me as a young person trying to figure out why in the world our lives fell apart in eighteen months. She stood strong. That doesn't mean she didn't cry or that she didn't have bad days, and we did have hurtful moments: You've got to be about 19 and share a one-bedroom apartment with your mother! *That's a lot of fun!* We had some moments, but in all of that still I would watch her with her Bible open reading late at night. I would hear her praying on her knees and I knew there was a real genuine relationship with a living God in her that would sustain. I finally came to a place in my life where I thought, "If this is working for Mama, it must be real." You finally give in and say, "I don't know why things happen like they do, but I'm going to get beyond the circumstance and just find relationship with somebody who can help me get through it."

I try not to cry. I tell this story four and five times a week in front of thousands or in front of three or four. I believe this testimony is why God has placed me where I am. I wish I didn't have this testimony. I'd rather have another one. I'd rather have all my sisters here and have us doing some stand-up routine together, but this is my story. Everytime I tell it I cry. I don't know why that is. Either some therapist someday is going to give me their card or it is just so *tender* and precious because when I hear the words, I see the pictures in my head. To express those to someone else is not only seeing sweet sights and sounds, but it's also the affirmation of how far God has brought me and how much I have seen and been through, and yet how faithful He was through every sight and scene that I'm expressing to someone. That is an affirmation to me every time so I can't help but cry in thanksgiving to His faithfulness in the toughest days.

Sometimes struggles are external events. They happen to us, and we try to deal with them as best we can. Sometimes they are happening inside of us, and we need to know there is hope.

David Meece

The most important thing for all human beings is to know God. I think that's what God wants for us more than anything—for us to know Him more. It's not to create gigantic ministries, it's not to do gigantic concerts, or to become famous, it's to know Him more.

My music, my keyboard, my piano playing were how I spoke as I expressed myself. But there came a time when God said, "Okay, David, it's time for you to grow. It's time for you to realize that's there's much more to life than what you've seen so far." It's a little scary when God says that because life can be very, very difficult. Life can be very, very hard even for the Christian. Sometimes even more so, because when Christians really get in touch with themselves and with what's going on around them and what God is doing, they hurt even more because they realize just how much they're missing here on this fallen planet.

My father passed away in 1986, and I realized after he died a lot of things I'd never faced. My piano was always my life, it's how I communicated with people, it's how I kept going. But my father's alcoholism was something I'd never dealt with. The physical abuse he threw on my mother was something I'd never dealt with. *You know, when you're a ten-year-old kid and you watch your dad trying to kill your mother, it does things to you.* What happens most the time, and in the case of my brother, my sister, and me, is that we shut down. We didn't want to face those kinds of things, we didn't want to see those kinds of things. It's too painful. My father tried to kill everyone in my family one night. He had a gun, and he was rounding everybody up; he was going to kill everybody. We were able to get the gun from him and call the police, and they carried him away. I was maybe 11 years old, and it was the last time I saw my father alive. The last two words he said to me were, "You're worthless."

The impact of that kind of thing can be profound. Most people tell you, "Just forget about it, keep going, you'll do better." Unfortunately, time doesn't always heal. Sometimes the wound is so deep that you really need to go back and face these things and work through them in a realistic fashion using God's word, prayer, and God's people. That's what the Church is for. That's what the Holy Spirit is for. Ultimately, I knew I had to get over this kind of thing because I had developed over the years—deep, deep inside—a deep hatred for my father for what he did to my mom. I was finally able to forgive him in 1988. The album *Learning to Trust* really summed up the *process* I went through.

Christianity is a process. It's not that you become a Christian, and then it's over. Life is a process; you grow and you change. Sometimes it's two steps forward, three steps back. Fortunately, if you're a Christian, the Lord calls you, saying, "Hey, Dave, up here. Let's try this other route. Come on with Me."

There is light at the end of the tunnel. There is hope. Yes, it's hard, and, yes, sometimes you fall down, and, man, you just don't know if you can get back up again. Sometimes you have the urge just to give up. You've had all this happen to you when you were just a child. I've talked to people who have been sexually abused, physically abused, and emotionally abused. I've talked to people who are going through battered spousal stages and all this kind of thing. It thrills me to be able to say to them, "Hang in there; it does get better." We'll always struggle, but it will get better.

When asked if he was thinking a lot about heaven these days, Bryan Duncan gave this answer in regard to his song "Dying to Meet You."

Bryan Duncan

I'm thinking a lot about death. Because ultimately, it is the big test. It started to change my life back on the *Mercy* album days when I wrote a song called "You Don't Leave Me Lonely." Originally, it was, "*You*, Don't Leave Me Lonely!" It was like I was screaming at God, "Don't leave me like this!"

I really need to know if this is true. And I remember at the funeral of a 10-year-old friend of my son's, being at the grave site and having the pastor staring at the grass for a good couple of minutes. He finally looks up and says, "I guess this is the real litmus test isn't it? We expect to bury our parents, but we don't expect to bury our kids."

It was like the beginning of an overwelming sense of impending doom. That I couldn't stop my own life from ending, I couldn't stop anybody else's life from ending, and it really gripped me. I thought about a lot of things. I haven't stopped thinking about death. I would imagine from even childhood growing up in church, every Sunday was, "Where will you spend your eternal destiny?"

So before I was a year old I was probably panicked about dying, almost so panicked that I couldn't live.

So all I'm doing is trying to get a handle on how to approach death. It's time to get ahold of that as far as I'm concerned. It's just scary, that's all. There's part of me that says, "Great, I'm going to meet God someday," but then I say, "Hey, what if the whole thing's backward? What if I have no clue?" It's the anticipation and it's mixed with all kinds of anxiety and fear and the sense that you have to leave everybody and you have to do that yourself. Woody Allen said, "I don't mind dying, I just don't want to be there when it happens."

I think the best part of that song ["Dying to Meet You"] is that it says, "Like streaks of gold and purple in the morning sky." It needs to be that kind of approach, I think, about dying and about meeting your Maker. It's the dark and the light contrasts that make it such a beautiful picture. If it wasn't for the dark, you wouldn't see how gorgeous the light was. I can live with the streaks of fear and uncertainty about the end of my life if I can see it like the sunrise that it will literally catch my breath. If I can imagine leaving this world like that. Like when I was talking about the sea turtles in the ocean where they just take your breath away. You know, that would be the best way to leave the earth—to realize when I stop breathing I'm going to see God face to face. That will take my breath away.

Through the years we have heard many difficult stories from Christian artists on a wide range of subjects. Without exception, the storyteller always finds the silver lining. Faith strengthens them and ourselves as well. In this story, Bruce Carroll is offered a position to lead praise and worship in another state. Sometimes turning a page of life literally means no turning back.

Bruce Carroll

We had prayed through the possible move and whether or not I was to take this position at this church. We felt peace about it and felt like God was leading us here. Then we went and got some bids by some moving companies and went through that whole process. I had never used a professional moving company to move my entire household, so I had no experience. And it was not a pleasant experience.

They never made it out here. We were at the house and waiting for the truck when I got a call from their headquarters. They called and said, *"Hey, your stuff caught fire in Kansas, and the load is a total loss."* It was a real drag to hear that because we lost a lot of stuff. It's really thrown our lives in turmoil. It's difficult to start pretty much over from scratch. I felt bad for my kids and my wife more than for me. But, I really sensed that in a strange sort of way, that it was just confirmation that we were doing the right thing. All of my friends, I mean the people that I've really been accountable to for years and that I've allowed to speak into my life, they all felt the same thing. Like, "Man, this is just an attack from the enemy because you're entering into the praise and worship realm—and we all know how the enemy feels about that." What else can he do short of taking one of your children or your wife or a family member to totally disrupt your life? I mean think about it.

So I just got a lot of strength in a God sort of way that "this too shall pass," and we're going to get through it. This is just confirmation that God wants us to do exactly what we're doing. People have rallied around us and the church has been great about meeting some of our immediate needs. God has been incredibly faithful and it's given me a lot of pretty neat opportunities to minister in a new and deeper way.

I have learned that stuff will burn. Stuff that you can't imagine burning burns. That's why we definitely need to put our hope and our trust in things that don't burn. The only thing that is eternal, hopefully all of us know, is the reality relationship that we have with Christ and the hope of glory.

I'm not saying that it didn't hack me off and that I didn't go through extreme anger and resentment and bitterness. As we speak, I've got an attorney. We're duking it out because they don't want to settle with me. You know, it's just been a nightmare on Elm Street. But through it all, I'm not going to lose my zeal. I'm not going to lose my excitement for the work that's going on out here. I'm not going to lose my excitement for what God is doing in the lives of me and my family. That's God because that is not me. The old Bruce would have marched straight to the headquarters and grabbed somebody by the neck and pounded them. But God is alive and well, and I just thank Him that's He's given me enough grace not to do that and to let it go.

After Andy Denton's group Legend Seven disbanded, he was left without a recording contract, work, or income. What do you do when one passage of life has ended and there's uncertainty about what is next?

Identical Strangers

(Andy Denton, Randy Thomas)

Andy: At first it's kind of scary because you don't know what the future holds, but you have to hold on to the fact that He does.

That was a time where I really had to just give up and just say, "God, whatever You want me to do, I'll do."

When I got out of Legend, I ended up just working at my church and working at the YMCA. I was doing things that some days I would wake up and tell my wife, *"This is so hard. This is so humbling."* I was used to playing music, doing live concerts, and making records. Then all of a sudden it wasn't there anymore, and I wondered if I'd ever do music again.

I think God just brought me to the point where I had to say, "Okay, if I never do that again . . . *please change the desires of my heart.*" That was one of my prayers, because I think music is in my blood. It's just something I've always had. I felt that was the assignment God had placed on my life.

I've come to a place now where I'm saying God has *not called me to be a musician.* God has called me to a relationship with Christ. That's my calling. Now from there, God assigns us to what we do. There are blessings and the offspring of being obedient to Him and having that relationship with Christ.

That's a hard thing. I think when I first became a Christian, it was, "Oh, God's called me to do music." Well, you can get all wrapped up. If that's who you become, it's going to be a short-lived thing. But if our foundation and our relationship are built on Christ, then all these experiences are going to be wonderful things.

So I'm standing here saying it's been a wonderful experience going through that humbling time. My wife said to me one day when I was still doing the humbling work, "You know I respect you more right now than I've ever respected you before, because you were obedient to God, and you proved to me that you care more about our family than you do about yourself." And I wept just because I thought, *Thank You God that my wife senses something in me that I didn't know if anybody would ever see.*

When you're drawn *out* of what you love and God gives you the opportunity to do it again, it's even that much sweeter. I truly believe God has had His hand on Identical Strangers from the very beginning.

For all the anguish we experience, wishing we could turn back time and change someone's path when they lose control, enjoy this story. All of the ingredients are there for crash and burn, but here the story is different, the ending is changed, and the life is turned around.

Brent Bourgeois

I was in Bourgeois-Tagg, a band that my partner Larry Tagg and I formed in the mid-eighties. We had a nice string of success that was really culminated by the song, "I Don't Mind At All." Through that song we were MTV favorites at that time and went on *The Tonight Show*, *American Bandstand*, and toured pretty much the whole world. We opened for people like Robert Palmer and Heart. It was nice. During that time things materialistically get better and better, so it's hard to see yourself getting worse and worse. But at the end of the second record, I had lost personal control of my life and I knew it. It was a great moment of clarity. Thank God that I did, because my wife and I were expecting our first child.

The catalyst for this was, we were being produced by Todd Rundgren, and I was driving him home one night from the studio toward the end of the record. I got pulled over for drunk driving. I ended up spending the night in jail in the drunk tank.

I think the thing that struck me that night was how many times, probably a thousand times, that I had been many times more drunk than I was that night and had been driving. That night I was actually sober enough to come to terms with that. I had been so much worse so many more times and been in the car driving.

I was definitely sober enough to have some serious thinking going on. I really realized at that moment, *This is what it's come down to, and thank God it's only come to this because it could have been so much worse.* I mean, I didn't kill anybody, I wasn't dead, I hadn't lost my wife or my house. But these things I could see were all coming; it just was a matter of time. This was a big marker—here I was, in jail. It was just a matter of time before the next thing happened.

The other thing that came to my attention at that time was that I couldn't perform normal functions in my life without having to go somewhere and get drugs to do it. In order to go to a movie, I had to first go to a drug dealer's house, get some drugs, and then go to a movie. Life had kind of come to that. It got to the point where I wasn't doing drugs anymore, they were doing me. They were controlling my timetable—where I went, how long I stayed, if I could even go, certainly when I went to bed and when I got up. It was really a fifteen-year struggle because I started playing music so young in bars, which was musically a good thing, but socially almost a tragic thing.

[The song "I Don't Mind At All"] was really kind of at the end of the road as well as another song that was on my first solo record which was called, "Can't Feel the Pain." Those two songs really were me at the end of my rope. I think sometimes how different my life would have been if we hadn't been expecting a child. But God puts things in your life when He does. I think it's marvelous, His rhythm.

My management at that time, sneaky as they were, got me a lawyer who was a member of a twelve-step program.

She sort of got me twelve-stepped along the way. It was a great serendipitous occurrence because it happened at exactly at the right time. I was ready to stop, but I needed someone to just give me that push down the hill. That was exactly what I needed when I needed it.

By 1987, the list of casualties in the music business was long. I was bloated and had lost control. I'm a control person, and I had lost my ability to say no. By then, I had enough of the Christian faith in me to help me turn around. I had been with Charlie Peacock, working with him since before and after his transformation, and it was a great inspiration to me. I started being envious of the turnaround in his life. At that point, when you're enslaved by drugs and alcohol, you're a great taker of things. You'll suck everything you can out of everybody around you because you need, you need, you need, and it's not a whole lot about giving anything. When I saw Charlie sober and going to church, getting his life back together, something in my head wanted to take that out of him too. I wanted that, I wanted what he had, and I wanted it right then. It seemed to me if he could do it, I could do it.

One of the funny things now (although it wasn't funny then), was that Charlie got sober and saved a couple of years before I did. Occasionally, we still would work together. After he got clean and sober, he was producing commercials. He'd call me and some other people to sing on them or play on them. *He'd call these sessions at 9:00 in the morning, and we used to think he was nuts!* How could *anybody* do anything at 9:00 in the morning, I mean other than birds? I can remember that very clearly, being very upset at him for having the nerve to get anybody to do music at 9:00 in the morning. The funny thing is that now, 9:00 in the morning is my best time. There's no other time of the day that I feel more alert and creative and ready to work than 9:00 in the morning.

This is a story of good wrapped up somewhere inside the struggle. Apart from everything that happens to The Martins, they endure. The strength of their family, the support of their friends, and their faith in God support them through the storms of life.

The Martins

(Joyce Martin, Jonathan Martin, Judy Martin)

Joyce: We grew up way out in the country in a place called Extra Community, Arkansas. It was way out in the middle of nowhere. We lived on the land that had been in my dad's family for years, in a house that had no electricity and no running water. It was there—without the influence of television or radio—that we learned how to sing. Looking back on it now, I guess it was just something to do. We had chores, schoolwork, and all that kind of thing—a fairly normal family life—except added to that the element of music: *Christian music* because Mom and Dad were both believers. We went to a little country church, and they encouraged us to sing.

There was a fireplace in the living room, and in the wintertime Mom and Dad would sleep in the living room. We would sleep in the room right off of it. I can remember we would wear coats to bed—I mean, it was cold! We had cracks in the walls and in the floors. You could see daylight. Mom would stuff sheets in the cracks. It would be as cold on the inside as it was on the outside. Especially when we would go off to church and the fire would go out. By the time you got home it would be cold again. My grandmother made us all quilts one year. All of us had individual-size quilts, you know the little, small kind? We would take those quilts and stand in front of the fireplace and get them really warm and wrap up in them and run and get in the bed. All three of us would sleep together a lot of times just to stay warm.

Judy: We also had a wood cookstove. In the wintertime it was great because you could be in the kitchen and stay warm. Now the smell of wood burning is just such a special part of my Christmases because it was something we grew up with.

Jonathan: And the smell of cedar trees. One of our highlights of Christmas was Daddy going hunting for a Christmas tree. We'd all line up in single file, Momma and Daddy and little duckies on the back. We'd walk out through the woods and find a nice cedar tree that was growing in an opening somewhere that was beautifully shaped. Dad would say, "*Is this the one?*" and we'd say, "*Yeah, Daddy, that's it!*" He'd cut it down and we'd drag it home, just so proud of that tree. That smell you just never forget.

Joyce: And we made our own decorations.

Jonathan: Tin foil on paper plates. Popcorn strings.

Joyce: We loved the encyclopedia and saw a picture of some little girls from Austria who'd put candles on their tree. We wanted to put candles on it, but my dad wouldn't let us because he was afraid we'd burn the house down!

Judy: It definitely didn't feel like we were without things, because we had clothes and food. I don't remember there ever being a time when we were really afraid that we might not have a meal. We definitely weren't poverty. Now, of course being grown, we understand the things that our mom and dad went without. We understand that there were things they dealt with that you never understand as children.

Joyce: Our community was a fairly poor community. It was a fairly small town and most of the people who worked there either worked at the mill in Crossett or did what their parents did in small little grocery stores and plumbing businesses. So we weren't a lot different from a lot of the people we associated with. Being without electricity was a choice that Mom and Dad made out of wisdom that I guess God gave them so that they could save money, a little bit along, to build a new house out in the country. And like Judy said, they may have been poorer than we remember, but we have wonderful memories.

Jonathan: It was my dad's dream to build a house for his wife. After three-and-a-half years of living without electricity, we did build that home. My mom actually drew the blueprints. She just knew everything she wanted in a home. We had a friend who was a contractor, and he came out with a couple of other guys, and they built it.

I remember moving in. The old house sat right in front of what we called "the big house." All we had to do was just carry our stuff from one house across the yard to the other. The electric company came and we paid to have electricity back there. For the longest time the electricity just came to the pole!

Judy: We would go to the tree and blow-dry our hair!

Jonathan: It was a Green Acres kind of thing; *climb up the pole to use the phone.* We would go to the light pole and dry our hair, and it was "*Woo-hoo!*"

Joyce: I remember the old refrigerator was the kerosene type.

Jonathan: There was a flame on the bottom that heated the freon, and the freon went up the coils in the back and got cold.

Joyce: The space was real limited in that refrigerator and so we couldn't have a lot of stuff in there. Boy when we got that new house we had *ice cubes!*

Jonathan: We ate everything cold!

Joyce: Oh man!

Judy: *"Don't heat up that hot dog, we want it cold!"*

Jonathan: It was a very nice experience to see Mom and how proud she was. We lived there a few years, and then dad just had circumstances in his life. He was our main source of income as a crop duster. He only flies during the farming season anyway, March through October, and he lost half of that season for three years in a row. So it became very hard on us financially.

I remember them calling us to the living room and sitting us down. Mom and Dad said, "We can't pay for this house because of these circumstances that have happened." Being teenagers in school, we didn't realize what a toll it was taking on our finances. They told us, "The bank will take this house back, and they'll have to sell it, and someone else will move back here. We're going to have to move back into the little house, and it can't stay on this piece of land because it goes with the big house. We have to move it out into the field."

The bank allowed us to stay in the house through Christmas. After Christmas was over, we had to move out because they were foreclosing.

Joyce: I think Mom and Dad asked them to.

Jonathan: Right, they did. They said, "Well, Christmas is coming. We haven't got a lot for the kids anyway. Could we at least stay in the warm house through Christmas?" I remember us having a Christmas, but it was a bittersweet holiday season that year. Christmas is something you can always find joy in, but in the back of our minds we knew that we were moving out. So it was very hard, a very hard Christmas.

Joyce: I was in high school, and I had this big bulletin board that had all the pep rally ribbons, the chrysanthemums, and all the memories that I had in school. I can remember the wind blowing really hard the day that I walked that bulletin board with everything on it across that field to go to that little house. We had all had our own rooms, but began to share a bedroom again. It was a sad day.

I remember also sitting in history class the day or two after we had moved back, and *flowers* came for me. I never got flowers at school unless my grandma sent me something for my birthday. Instead of asking me to go down to the office, the principal had them bring the flowers down to the room. I couldn't imagine who in the world would bring me flowers. But my friends had sent them to me. They were for my housewarming, for moving. I lost it, of course; I'm emotional anyway. The teacher let us all go outside, me and my three best friends. They had pitched in together and bought me roses because they knew it was a hard time for me.

Jonathan: We lived in the small house again for about five years. We did put in electricity. For a while we still bathed in a washtub. We used a woodstove again until we got the appliances bought or borrowed from family and neighbors.

Judy: When we moved back into the small house it was a year and a half before we got a bathroom put in. Our church family pitched in together, and they came out one Saturday and they spent the whole day putting in a septic tank and a bathroom.

Jonathan: Later Joyce got married and moved to Little Rock. We were traveling a lot then, so Judy and I decided, being single at the time, to move up there. After being there for three-and-a-half years, Harry [Joyce's husband] became a full-time part of our ministry.

Joyce: Jonathan had gotten married in the meantime, and we started praying for a way to cut back on our expenses so that Melinda [Jonathan's wife] could be a full-time part of our ministry as well. We just needed to save a little more money. We started packing sandwiches and stuff in the van instead of eating out and just cutting back on everything we could think to cut back on, and the last expense was *living expenses.*

We were all paying rent in three different houses. We thought, *If we could find one house where we could pitch in and pay rent and live together until we get back on our feet. If we could do that and live somewhere that the living expenses aren't as expensive as they are here in Little Rock.* So we just started praying and left it up to God. Mom and Dad were praying for us; they knew what we wanted to do.

The gentleman that had bought the house, the big house from the bank, called my dad one night and said, "I know your kids are wanting to move, and we're ready to sell this house. Do you think they'd be interested in buying this back?" My dad said, "Hold on one minute. I think I know the answer, but I'll call them." He called us, and we were just dancing with joy! We knew it was an answer to prayer. We moved back there. Mom and Dad went in with us, and we bought the house. We had enough money collectively to pay a down payment on the house and the land, and we started making payments together on this house until Mom and Dad were able to move back into that house. Now Mom works full-time for our ministry, and my dad's still flying.

God did that in a sentimental way. We knew He was going to provide. We knew there was somewhere for us to live and somewhere He was going to make it easier for us financially, but only God would have the heart and the desire to do it in a way that would be that special to us.

It's hard enough to outlast the conflicts that we face in life. When we give scorn instead of help to those who need our support, we sow seeds of bitterness in the lives of those depending on us. Sarah Jahn's story is for all of us who can't heal ourselves.

Sarah Jahn

The song "Chronic" was written for my mother. She has had Chronic Fatigue Syndrome for six years now. It's been a daily struggle. She has a lack of energy, experiences a lot of pain, and feels like she's not useful in the family. She's not able to work and not able to do a lot of things that it seems a mother should do. She's not able to go to functions or family reunions.

She's gone to a lot of doctors and tried a lot of treatments for this. I think doctors don't really know about Chronic Fatigue Syndrome, and they're kind of embarrassed when there's a case where they can't see any improvement. They don't really know what to do, and they just send her on her way. She's had a lot of people pray over her. My family believes in healing. My brother was healed from leukemia when he was 3 years old. He's now 21 years old, and he's not in remission—he's just completely healed. It's a real struggle for the family as well. Because we do believe in healing, there's been so much prayer about why she still has this. She's had a lot of hurtful comments from people trying to make sense of it. Like "maybe you don't have enough faith" or "maybe you're not praying in the right way." You know they can say their little thing and go on their way, but the next day she still has to live with it. She really wants to be healed.

People who've heard the song and have some kind of chronic problem, or have a family member who does, identify with this song immediately. They don't need to hear an explanation for the song. Other people ask what it's about. But some people come up to me after the show and they say, "I know exactly what that's about. I have Chronic Fatigue Syndrome, and you sang what I'm feeling."

The last few lyrics are: *"I can't heal myself, I can't heal myself, I can't heal myself."* I think that is a really important message. As humans, it takes getting to that level where we realize there isn't anything we can do to fix ourselves before we can really let Christ into our lives. And so this song is not the happy ending song. This song is not the answer song. This song is the moment right before the answer: that moment of despair when you realize there isn't anything you can do.

There are a lot of self-help programs out there and a lot of literature that you can buy to help problems like alcoholism, addictions, and different ailments. But if we're humanistic in our approach, then we still have the biggest problem of all—the fact that we're born into this sinful human nature. There isn't anything we can do about it. That's why we need a Savior.

These kinds of stories aren't happening just in the Christian music world. They go on in our worlds as well. Where can we turn when we need someone to lean on?

10 HOW TO SHOCK SOCCER MOMS AND BE A B.M.O.C.

> **"Connecting is not the only necessary ingredient in powerful relating, but it is central. It is the core good news of the gospel. Why? It's what we most want, what we most lack, what we most fear will never be ours."**
>
> **Dr. Larry Crabb**

INTERVIEW IS REALLY JUST CONVERSATION. Two people meet, shake hands, and begin to talk and connect with one another. Connecting, to me, is the proverbial meaning of life. It's perfectly shocking to those of us who actually *like* this sort of thing (some of us even do it for a living) that others, in fact, do not like it at all.

Much to their dismay, this chapter is about connecting. It's about Christians reaching out to others. It's a "how-to" discussion on becoming real with the people around you. By reading examples from the lives of these Christian artists, I hope we're challenged to be more prayerful and to draw strength from other believers. It's about how we all can help bring others closer to God, even if we can't sing.

If we're moved by the testimonies of Christian artists in this book, let's share our own faith, hearts, and testimonies with the people in our lives. Artists have a creative approach to serving Christ and the Church. But we can all find our own ministry by humbling ourselves before God and telling our own stories about His love for us.

One of the primary reasons why music has been so influential in generation after generation during the last forty years is that it connects one soul to another. What will happen to us if we choose to share with others the burdens in our own hearts and lives? What will happen to our churches, our families, our friendships? We're happy to hear Joe tell us about his new job, Helen's vacation to the Virgin Islands, and Al's incident with the wisenheimer waiter. But we recognize this as just chatter. Can Joe tell us about his father's alcoholism? When does Helen share about her rocky marriage? Or Al his depression and fears? These kinds of stories don't fit in as well in the break room. They don't really come up at family gatherings (not counting gossip), and we're lucky if we have someone with whom they come up at all. If we are not connected to friends or family, then where will we find intimacy?

The secret of shocking soccer moms and becoming a B.M.O.C. is to share Christ, who is now in you, with your world. It's what this book is about, what Christian music is about, and, most important, what life is about.

Rich Mullins

> I was talking to a friend of mine and he said, "You know, I just don't like Christians. I believe in Jesus and all that stuff, but I just hate hanging out with Christians." I said, "Yeah? You and me are friends, and I'm a Christian." He said, "Yeah, you're different." I said, "Well, I'll take that as a compliment, but I'm not sure what else you mean."
>
> I began to name several people that he knew who were Christians and eventually what we came around to in the conversation was—what he didn't like was—he didn't really know most Christians. A lot of the people that he went to church with alienated him. All he knew about them was what they believed, what picket lines they were going to stand on, whether or not they were literalists in their interpretation of Scripture. They all had a lot of doctrinal

positions: I am a nonsmoker. I am a teetotaler. I am a *whatever*. They all knew their place on a number of moral issues, but none of them were able to communicate who they were to him, so they seemed very boring and I can understand that. They seemed like non-people, like chess pieces.

I think one thing that is threatening to a good many of us is that we think, *If people really knew me they'd never believe in Jesus*. And I want to say, "No, that's exactly wrong." People will never know Jesus as long as we choose to hide ourselves. I don't think that necessarily means I need to go out and get on the radio to announce my private sins. I think that I can be very honest without being hurtful to people. What I think will please God is if I have progressed to being that person whose name is written on that white stone that He will give me.

Rich Mullins' words challenge us to live honestly in front of others. Or are we simply "chess pieces" standing at attention, never showing weakness?

We need to see how God's work is going on around us at all times. Amy Morriss tells us about the importance of listening for the sound of God's voice. It may prepare us for the girl who has waited when everyone else has gone.

Amy Morriss

I full well believe that for today, this is what the Lord is telling me to do. I don't know what He's going to tell me to do tomorrow or next week. I believe God is working all the time all over the place. That goes back to being able to hear His voice, being obedient to Him and in a right relationship with Him. I want to be able to hear what He says to me. I don't know how He's going to use me or where He's going to use me, but for some reason, He wants to use His children. Whatever that means tomorrow, if it's the same thing, wonderful.

After a concert I always stay until the last person has gone who wants to talk to me or pray or whatever. One time everyone else was gone except this one girl, and she had waited through everything. I went back into the auditorium, and we were sitting down talking. She just had a lot of things in her life—the devil was playing tricks with her mind and just really trying to confuse her. She had a lot of really unfortunate and terrible things that had happened in her life. She just couldn't understand if there was a God, why would He allow these terrible things to happen?

It was probably the most emotional, intense experience I've ever had talking and praying with someone before because I really believe the devil had completely blinded her. It was obvious that the Lord was working on her because, first of all, she was there. She'd never been in a church or in a Christian music situation ever before. A Christian friend of hers begged her and begged her to come. She ended up coming, and the Lord was just dealing with her, and she wanted so bad to take hold of Him. She wanted to so bad, but the devil kept lying to her, and she kept fighting it.

I prayed with her, but I really don't know what happened. I stayed with her well over an hour, and I called the pastor over there, and we prayed with her. I don't know what happened, but I'll never forget the experience because it was the first concert where I left there just crying my eyes out. I got on the bus and the guys from the band and all the sound people were on there, and they couldn't figure out what was going on. It was one of those things where all you could do was just say, "Lord, I don't even know this girl, but I know You're working in her and around her." I'd give anything if I knew how to get in contact with her some way, somehow, but I really believe the Lord planted a seed in her that night. I hope that she accepted Him as her Savior as some point, or, if she hasn't, that she will.

That's another reason why being obedient to the Lord and what He tells you to do is so important. Whether your ministry is working in an office sitting at a desk or whatever, it's so important to be obedient to Him, because there are people out there who are just crying out for help. They don't know that it's God they're looking for. Sometimes they do, sometimes they don't.

I don't know what has happened to her, but I know that the Lord hears my prayers, and I know that He's going to take care of her. He's going to do everything that He can to draw her to Him if she's open and willing to listen to Him.

It's shocking how two total strangers can have such a meaningful interaction. Something must have happened during that concert that made the girl stick around for some one-on-one time. I believe if we are a light, we will experience meaningful interactions with our audiences too—the people surrounding us.

Chonda Pierce told us that church is where we should be able to be ourselves and reach out to one another for support.

Chonda Pierce

Isn't it funny that the church sometimes is the place we're least allowed to speak the truth? I love the verse that says, "Ye shall know the truth and the truth will set you free." I think it not only speaks for Jesus Christ, the Way, the Truth, and the Life; He is the Truth, and His salvation has set me free. You know, Salvation is the most liberating thing in the whole wide world. I also think it means when you speak the truth, when you say, "You know, this was really crumby what happened to me." There's something very liberating and there's some freedom that comes from letting that out. So of all places to be able to get that out, we should be able to do that at church. We should speak truthfully in a healthy way; don't go up to sister so-and-so and say, "*I really hate your hair.*" But to really just say, "Here are some things I'm confused about. Why do people die? Why do people suffer? Why are there hungry kids in the world?" It's okay to have those questions.

I had a wonderful counselor tell me one time (and my mother will hate me telling this), but I remember sitting on the couch, and she said, "You know, Jesus really does love you. Have you ever embraced how much He really loves you in all of this?" I said, "No, as a matter of fact, if He walked in, I'd probably slap Him." That's how bitter and hurt I was that life had turned out like it had. She said, "And you know what, He'd let you. He'd let you slap the other side, and when you got all through with your [little] fit, then He'd wrap His arms around you because that's how much He loves you." Well, it blew me away! To know that there is no question that He can't handle. There's no anger that He won't still love you for. There is nothing that you can do that will separate you from the love of God. That was so liberating. To find out what grace really was in my life. That it is okay to have a sense of humor. That it's okay to be the middle child and want to stick out like a sore thumb. And it's alright to hurt now and then and to be angry about it. The Truth will set you free.

Connection exists when two writers get together to talk on an intimate level about what their songs ought to say. When writing the song, "What Kind of Love," artist Chris Eaton teamed up with Amy Grant. Their writing session began by checking in with their own deep conditions of the heart.

Chris Eaton

On one beautiful sunny morning I traveled to Riverstone farm to see Amy. Whenever I come into town I try to contact her and just see how she's doing. Sometimes we get to write stuff together and sometimes we don't. Obviously, it depends on her schedule, but on this occasion she said, "Come over, I really want to write." So of course I was there in a minute, and we just sat around her piano and started discussing different thoughts and ideas like we normally do, just bouncing them off each other. I'd had the chorus in my head [which asked]: *What kind of love is a love that won't let me down?* Exactly what kind of love is this that deals with us in a way that we don't deal with one another? That continually allows us back home? The prodigal love. What kind of a love allows us to make mistakes and still loves us? And why is there not enough of that love in each other? Why don't we treat each other that way?

There are times when all of us as Christians just throw our hands up in the air and say, *What the heck is going on? Where is God in all of this? Why am I so unable to tap into that purity and holiness on a regular basis?*

There are times when you just need to sit down and just share stuff with people over a cup of coffee and say, "This is happening to me. My life's changing. I've got a new job. You've got a baby on the way, you didn't know that was going to happen. Where is God in all this? Where do we go next? We need each other." It's just simple things like that. Being able to show your heart to your deepest friend. Not wearing your heart on your sleeve for everybody who comes along—that's not good either. I think protection of your heart is a really important thing which I'm learning now—but there are choices we have to make. Sometimes it's difficult to hold on to the truth, but that's the only thing we have to hold on to. There's are times when we're hurting, and in our own walk with God we may find it difficult to believe that God has got the answer. So we need to go to someone else who will sit and go, "Hey, it's okay. He's still here. He still loves you." *We need that. We need each other.* But the song ["What Kind of Love"] just kind of happened, and Amy put her very distinctive lyric in it which made it very personal and more friendship based. That's what that song's about.

Sarah Gaines shared this story about meeting up with women after a concert who wanted to know if life is easier for Christians in the limelight. The exchange that took place is an encouragement to everyone.

Billy & Sarah Gaines

Sarah: I meet a lot of mothers whom I think about a lot and some of them I still talk to on the phone or we write letters. We talk about kids, teenagers, and the pressures that they go through, we talk about homeschooling, and just what God expects from us as mothers and wives. We talk about recipes too.

There is a strength that comes from sharing those things with people, because they don't know how we live at home, and they think that things are better off for us, that we don't deal with the same pressures and things that they deal with because we sing, but we do. We have children and we have things that we have to take care of like cleaning house, cooking, and trying to keep a schedule

> and, you know, just things that we all do. We talk about keeping a relationship with the Lord in the midst of all that. Learning to put Him first and seek Him first thing in the day, although you're tempted to do other things first. We talk about things like that, and we enjoy talking to each other about things because it makes them feel comfortable. It's encouraging to me, too, knowing that I go through the same things that they go through.

What's happening when we exchange the news of our lives with one another? We're fine-tuning ourselves to the goodness we find in people we like and want to be like. Rocketown, a youth dance club established by Michael W. Smith, became the place where outsiders could feel love and a sense of value. This monumental achievement is accomplished by the simple act of remembering names.

Michael W. Smith

> We're open three nights a week. Friday nights are pretty much the diehard night. I always refer to it as spiritual warfare night because for a while we got some pretty intense kids who came in on Fridays—alot of kids who are from dysfunctional families and really struggling. I believe they would come back every Friday because they felt like they had a home. Every staff member there, whether there were twenty or thirty staff, they all knew [these kids] by their names. Because they knew them, they loved them—didn't matter what they were into; they just loved them and established a relationship with them. I think that's a big reason why they came back and found a home at Rocketown.

You've heard it said that the people of God and the unrepentant world shouldn't mix. Perhaps you've been warned to stay away from worldly people so that you won't be influenced or spiritually harmed by them. Apparently, Andrae Crouch has missed this rule. He actually seeks them out.

Andrae Crouch

I remember a long time ago at the National Quartet Convention, a lot of people were putting down Elvis, saying he was only about "shake, shake, shake" and moving his body. He had just recorded one of my songs, "I've Got Confidence." Somebody took me into his trailer and introduced me to him. I think the group The Imperials were singing with him at the time. He said, "Glad to meet you," and he said he liked the song and things like that. But nobody in this big convention center knew he was there. A lot of people I knew, if they would have even heard of me sitting with him they would have called me everything but a child of God. But when they announced that Elvis was in the room, and he came up on the platform, that place went crazy! People ran. I mean pastors' wives, pastors' children, and pastors ran up to that platform just to touch Elvis Presley. It was like a stampede.

I know what a lot of people say about a person like Michael Jackson. I feel if anyone should be around them it should be a Christian. I think what we have is so far greater and stronger than any demonic power that they could even possess. Greater is He who is within us, than he who is in the world affecting other people.

So when Michael Jackson asked me and his producer Quincy Jones to be involved, the first song that I worked on with him was "Man in the Mirror." First of all, I listened to the song, and I liked the words. I will never participate in something if I feel the lyrics or the content of the project is against what I believe in theologically or spiritually. I always check that out, and I have people who keep up with all the different *isms* of the religious world to make sure that I'm not validating something that I may not be aware of. Some little symbol, some little this or that. So I make sure that that happens before I get involved. I just think, *What better influence could people like Michael Jackson and Madonna have around them than the people I would be bringing in to help me do the project?* What better influence could they have than a bunch of praying people and a bunch of talented people and them being surrounded with people who will be praying for them?

So that's the reason I took on the project, regardless of what they've done. If a person would not want me to do that, they should also not want me to sing in a prison or on the street. Because everything is in the prison and everything is on the street. I believe that's where the Bible says go onto the highways and byways. Not because of what they believe, but because of what you believe and what you think can be done when they hear the gospel. I do believe that someday with all the prayers that have gone for Michael and for Madonna that in God's mercy He's going to draw them unto Himself. Is that a good answer? I think that's a great answer. Because where else are the most weird people and every demonic force than in a prison? And He said I want you to go to the prison. I was in prison, and you visited Me there. So I was in prison within myself, so a person like Michael Jackson might say. I was in prison in a studio; I was bound in sin and you came and saw Me. So that's my opportunity to visit people who are not behind bars but unknowingly are bound to sin.

Mark Lowry also gives us a great lesson in how to communicate with other people. Slip it into your pocket. You never know when you might need it.

Mark Lowry

The best way is through a story. Jesus did it that way. Everybody will listen to a story. *People* magazine is so popular because it is nothing but a compilation of stories about people. People love to hear about people. And they can always relate themselves to the story. I think the best sermons are preached when they're preached at ourselves: When I tell a story about me, about my childhood, about my life. In a song, I try not to use the word *you*. Like, *You should worship only at the feet of Jesus.* Keep it in the personal: *I will worship only at the feet of Jesus.* I keep it on *me*. Because people hear that, and it's not as in-your-face. It's "Oh, I see me in that. I get it now."

Your sermon can be full of great content, but if everybody's asleep by the time you say the final "amen," what good is it? It can be full of great theology and life-changing ideas, but if everybody's *snoring*, what good is it?! But when you take those great ideas and you put them in a story, whether it be a lyric, or just a monologue or a sermon, people walk away with something they can wear home.

"There are many, many testimonies" says Cameron Dante of The World Wide Message Tribe. There are many people who need what you as a Christian uniquely possess.

World Wide Message Tribe
(Cameron Dante, Andy Hawthorne)

Cameron: Many people have had their lives changed through God using this ministry. It really isn't about us; it's about God.

There are many, many testimonies, but one in particular sticks in my mind. When I was ministering in a school, one kid walked up to me on the Monday morning and they were just saying how stupid we were as Christians, so what were we doing in their lessons? There was a gang of them hanging around in the back of the classroom. Then we noticed at the next lesson two of these guys were still there. And then the next lesson. And then the next lesson. They were playing truant from all their lessons and kept staying in ours. Now we knew this was wrong, but these were the head guys of the school. You know, they weren't going for any teachers. They weren't going for us. So we just asked them if they'd stay nice and quiet and maybe sit at the back of the classroom.

But then Tuesday came, and they started making their way forward to the front of the class. Then Wednesday they were actually reserving front seats at the beginning of the classes we were taking. On the Friday, we were just about to do the evangelistic concert that night. But that day during the lessons, I asked them, "Why is it that you keep staying in this classroom?" And they said, "When we leave the classroom we feel as though something's missing. We know what you're saying is right, but when we leave the classroom we become scared."

So that Friday night, they both came to the evangelistic concert that The World Wide Message Tribe does, and they both gave their lives to Christ. Then on the Sunday, they both came to the Planet Life concert [a special Sunday service provided as a follow-up to the Friday night concert], and *they were worshiping God!* It's such a beautiful sight to see people that are worshiping God for the very first time. They're free. Free from all chains and all barriers, these guys just gave God His whole worth.

When I asked them why they wanted to be in the classroom while we were preaching the message of Jesus, they said it was this thing about being drawn to the light

> and being afraid of the darkness. They wanted to be where the light was, but they didn't feel they were strong enough when they left that classroom. They felt weak because they didn't feel they could take God out of that classroom and into real life and into day-to-day living. When they gave their lives to Christ and accepted the Holy Spirit, that day-to-day living became so much easier.

When we open our mouths to share what's going on in our lives, people can relate absolutely. They hear about the light that we speak of, and a hope in their hearts is quickened. When it is, you'll be the first to know.

Tuesday's Child

(Linda Elias, Lesley Glassford)

> **Linda:** People are pretty much the same wherever you go. Everybody's facing the same struggles and challenges that you're facing. I think it's encouraging for them to see that Lesley and I, though we're on a stage and are singing, we're really just saying the same things that they're feeling. We are just speakers of the songs. We communicate the song and the emotion of the song, and they are emotions that a lot of people feel. That's the great thing about music—it's got that ability to touch people in an amazing way. When you've got a song with a very deep lyrical content, it's that much more rewarding when it strikes a chord with somebody. It's like, "Okay, there is somebody else who's feeling this way. I'm okay, and I can get through it."
>
> **Lesley:** We are Christians. Our hearts have been given over to the Lord. So therefore, we write from a Christian perspective, and so when we write a song about a real-life, tough situation, hopefully we're not leaving people hanging at the end of it. In other words, we try to

express that life is hard and this has been a tough thing, but there's a ray of hope at the end because there is a God who does have the answer.

If we can bring a ray of hope into a song that really tackles a tough thing, then we've accomplished something. That person who comes up and says, "I've never heard any of this stuff! I've never heard that there's any kind of hope in the midst of the hell that I'm going through right now." That's the first step in us being able to reach out to them and let them know that there is hope and there's more to life than what they're experiencing.

Unless we ask we may never know what is going on in the lives of the people around us. Here's the story of the girl they only saw as the one who sang the solos and played the piano for the church group.

Lisa Bevill

I became a Christian when I was 9 years old. I was in a church every time the door was open: Wednesday night supper, Sunday morning, Sunday night. Our church had phenomenal youth outreach and an incredible youth group. I played piano for our church group, sang, and did solos. We went on youth retreats, and so I was very involved growing up.

A lot of things happened to me when I was growing up, and I don't talk about them to have a pity party, but I did go through some difficult things that shaped the person that I am and make me want to reach out to youth. I just remember so well never really fitting in. I never fit in because I felt like I was fat, I was ugly. I didn't know how to wear makeup. I was always wearing secondhand clothes. My mom worked at a consignment shop, so she was always giving me clothes from there.

But when I was twelve my mom was diagnosed with lymphoma, which is cancer of the lymph nodes. They are all over your body, so it totally affected her immune system. My dad as far back as I can remember always had really bad arthritis. It seemed like, for at least a span of eleven years, he was having an operation every single year either on his knees, or his hands, or his feet, or some part of his body. So I grew up seeing my parents always ill, in and out of the hospital.

I remember on Saturday afternoons ironing my dad's shirts for work the next week, washing the clothes, helping my brother take care of the lawn, and doing a lot of the cooking at night for my mom. That's just what I remember growing up. It wasn't until much, much later in my early twenties that I realized that my childhood was very different from everyone else's. I thought the life that I had lived was very normal. I thought that everybody my age dealt with these kinds of problems at home. That definitely shaped who I became.

I realized that as a youth, no one from the church really reached out to me and said, "Lisa, how are you dealing with this emotionally? What are you doing with all these feelings? Aren't you angry? Aren't you this, and aren't you that?" No one ever reached out to me that way. They were always reaching out to the parents who were ill and going through all the things, and the children were just sort of forgotten. And so it made all the teen issues that I was facing just that much bigger to me. I was very suicidal from 12 years on when my mom found out she had cancer. It was an open door for Satan to walk in and to play with my mind. *"You're not worth anything. Your parents are going to die!"*

And it just made me very suicidal, at least I thought about suicide. I don't think I would have ever gone through with it, but the thoughts were definitely there, that I amounted to nothing. That makes my heart a lot more tender toward kids because they are facing a whole lot more these days. Just with the things they face in school, the whole sexual pressure, issues of self-esteem, who's better than who, who's better-looking. I just remember all that. Those things are still fresh on my mind and on my heart.

Chonda Pierce is what's known affectionately as a "Preacher's Kid." Growing up in a church's "First Family" has innate pressures that have in many cases damaged the people in them. Peering into the past, present, and future of this story we begin to see the discomfort of being alone, then the curiosity and wonder of connection. Perhaps we can even see hope for the future as these P.K.s reach out to one another.

Chonda Pierce

When you travel like I do, you become like the Pied Piper. Preacher's Kids just come out of the woodwork and you don't know what to do with them. There are preacher's kids that, like I said earlier, just want to be heard. They just want someone to hear their side of the story. Sometimes it's funny. Sometimes it's stuff they've harbored for years and years that they can't let go of. Some of our denominations are doing really good about ministering to the pastor's family. We've come up with 1-800 numbers, counseling, and a realistic slant on what it's really like to give and give and give. That's really great, but for many who are "older" like me, we kind of missed the boat on that. The 800 number wasn't quite set up back then, so some of us have kind of slipped through the cracks, and so you run into people who are just longing to fellowship. A couple of years ago all I could think of was, "Let's just have a yearly party and see if anybody comes." So we started just getting the word out, putting little notes and flyers on our tables wherever we would go. Bryan [Duncan] would mention it from time to time, and I would, too, where I would go. Lo and behold, about 108 preacher's kids from all over the country showed up in Nashville. All denominations were there, and we didn't know what to expect. The incredible thing was standing on the balcony of this church that we used and watching people walk in and the looks that they had. They were looking at each other, checking each other out to see if this was a real safe place or not. And to watch them realize—many of them for the first time in their lives—that they were not alone. That we all got a little angry every now and then. That every once in awhile we all got our feelings hurt. That once in a blue moon something happened that disappointed us. And for the first time they went, "Man, I didn't know somebody else felt this way." It let them feel free to talk about the honesty that God knew, we just allowed them a place to verbalize. In that honesty we thought we'd better have some people who are really *good listeners* unlike Bryan and I (we just want to do all of the talking!). We had a couple of folks come in from Focus on the Family that came in to talk to us, men who were also preacher's kids and missionary's kids. From that first year material has been accumulated and data processed until a couple books have come out of those events. Now we have some literature that's more helpful—for people kinda stuck in their unforgiveness or people who don't see the sense of humor in all of it or people who haven't found God. So we're excited about it. We've been doing this now every year. It's been great.

To what better artist to give the last word? Steve Camp shared this story about his visit to the hospital room of an AIDS patient. In it, we learn not so much from Steve, but from the dying patient how to approach the physically and spiritually dying.

Steve Camp

In 1988 the Lord challenged my heart to start a ministry to people who have AIDS. This was done publicly through a soft, meek, calm, inhibited speaker named Tony Campolo. He subpoenaed my attention in front of two thousand people at the Gospel Music Association main gathering. I was the least likely candidate for this kind of spiritual leadership. In short order, an awareness organization was formed called AIDS Crisis and Christians Today (ACCT). Our banner was "His holiness not compromised; yet His mercy not restrained." We didn't condone homosexuality, bisexuality, promiscuity among heterosexuals, or illegal drug use. But at the same time we couldn't condone the self-righteous attitudes in much of the Church towards dying people who need the Savior, not our condemnation. During the few years that followed, we had the opportunity to see literally hundreds of men and women with AIDS repent of their sin and come to a saving knowledge of Jesus Christ—to know that even though their bodies were deteriorating, they could have hope in Christ for eternity; that nothing could separate them from the love of God in Christ Jesus our Lord; and that "to be absent from the body is to be present with the Lord."

Let me share one of those encounters with you. I had the chance after one of these awareness concerts to go visit a man in his hospital room who was unable to come to the concert. I was permitted by the staff there to talk with him for a brief time. Upon entering his room we shook hands, however, he would not let go of my hand. He kept squeezing it tighter and tighter, holding onto it and staring intensely at me. He finally said to me, after what seemed like several minutes but was, in reality, only a few seconds: "Listen, if you're going to be in my hospital room with me for awhile, look me in the eye." I was already looking him square in the eyes, but to mollify the tension I said, "Okay, I will." He then looked at me and asked, "Are you afraid of me?" "Afraid of what?" I asked. "I have AIDS," he responded. I answered "No, I'm not afraid of you—that's why I'm here." He continued to squeeze my hand tighter and tighter, and then, finally and much to my satisfaction, he let go. But then, I wouldn't let go of his hand—I started to tighten *my* grip. I looked at him and said, "Listen, if I'm going to be in this hospital room with you, look me in the eye." He started to smile a bit. I then asked, "Are you afraid of me?" "Afraid of what?" he blurted out. I said, *"I have a cold!"* He smiled and responded, "No, I'm not afraid of you." "Great," I said. "Now that we have the disease out of the way, my name is Steve. How are you?" He went on to say that no one had ever talked like that to him before. I said, "They should have, you're a very rude person." He responded, "You don't understand . . . I have AIDS." I informed him that the last time I looked, rudeness wasn't symptomatic of AIDS. He not only had a blood problem, but a heart problem as well. We needed to talk about both.

I had a wonderful opportunity to share the Lord with this man. We had a chance to talk for fifteen or twenty minutes. He asked why I was there. I gladly said that my faith demanded I be there. To stay away would be antithetical to the purpose of Christ and would prove that my love for the Lord was not genuine but a hypocritical love. I unfolded the gospel to him, but he did not respond. He was hard and embittered against the truth of God's Word and probably because of some of God's people. But before I left, he shared something that impacted my life forever, and I need to share it with you.

He told me that a few months earlier a group of about eight people walked into his hospital room. They laid their hands on him, said a quick prayer in some gibberish he didn't understand, and left. Apparently they just did their Christian "duty" and vamoosed. (It's called *guilt.*) He asked me if they were really Christians. I said I didn't know. Reflecting back on his encounter with them, he thought they were trying to heal him. I told him I didn't know, and I apologized for their behavior. I had to ask him though, "Did you want to be healed?" He said something I would never forget. Broken and embittered he uttered, "Steve, I'd rather be loved." He said, "People tell me all the time, 'Jesus loves you.'" What he wanted to know was when would one of us as Christians love him?

That's a penetrating, fair question. To think that someone is willing to live with their imminent life-threatening disease, rather than to be healed and live with religious hypocrisy.

I wrote a song out of that and other experiences called, "Don't Tell Them Jesus Loves Them 'Til You're Ready to Love Them Too." Jesus said that the greatest commandments are: Love the Lord your God with all your heart, soul, mind and strength . . . and love your neighbor as yourself.

It's so important for us, beloved, not just to tell people "Jesus loves you" and them casually give them a tract, a religious note, or catch phrase and walk away thinking we've really shared Christ. Nowhere are we commanded in Scripture "to go into all the world and hand out paper." We must give them the gospel *and* give them ourselves. We must expend our lives in serving and caring for them—and in doing so, point them to our great God and Savior Jesus Christ our Lord!

Our neighbor is anyone in our path in need. Will you love your neighbor for Christ's sake today?

COMPASSIONATE MINISTRIES

Mission of Mercy
P.O. Box 63600
Colorado Springs, CO 80962

Compassion International
Colorado Springs, CO 80997-0009

Mercy Ministries of America
P.O. Box 111060
Nashville, TN 37222-1060

World Vision
P.O. Box 688
Fayetteville, GA 30214

The Bible League
16801 Van Dam Road
South Holland, IL 60473

American Bible Society
1865 Broadway
New York, NY 10023-7505

Focus on the Family
Colorado Springs, CO 80995-7620

Feed the Children
Larry Jones International Ministries, INC
P.O. Box 36
Oklahoma City, OK 73101-0036

Food for the Hungry
P.O. Box 12349
Scottsdale, AZ 85267-9917

Youth with a Mission
P.O. Box 78219
Nashville, TN 37207

Message to Schools
P.O. Box 14
CHEADLE
Cheshire
SK8 2FE
United Kingdom

A Place in the Sun Camp for Girls
P.O. Box 210993
Nashville, TN 37221 Tele: 615-662-7913
(Lisa Bevill)

The Legacy of Kid Brothers of St. Frank
P.O. Box 11526
Wichita, KS 67202
(Rich Mullins)

Prison Fellowship Ministries
P.O. Box 97103
Washington, DC 20090-7103

HOW TO CONTACT SOUL2SOUL:

Soul2Soul
P.O. Box 2543
Brentwood, TN 37024

friends@s2sradio.com

ABOUT THE AUTHOR

Christopher Coppernoll has interviewed more than 125 Christian musicians for "Soul2Soul," a one-hour syndicated radio program heard weekly on over 330 Christian stations by more than 750,000 listeners. A songwriter himself, Coppernoll has more than 800 compositions to his credit. He has a music degree from the prestigious Berklee College of Music in Boston and resides in Franklin, Tennessee.